The Poet

The Poet

by

Vivian Shipley

Louisiana Literature Press
Hammond, Louisiana

Printed in the United States of America
FIRST EDITION, 2015

Cover Art: Marcia Ann Harris
Oil on canvas
33" by 45"
My Parents at Halloween
1971

Photograph of Cover Art by Todd Jokl
Author's Photo: Wayne Chapman

Requests for Permission to reproduce material from this work should be
sent to: Louisiana Literature Press
                SLU Box 10792
                Hammond, LA 70402

Acknowledgments

Grateful acknowledgment is made to the editors of the journals in which
these poems, often in earlier versions, first appeared: the *American Scholar,
Another Chicago Magazine, Arkansas Review,* the *Birmingham Poetry Review,
Blueline,* the *Briar Cliff Review, Calliope,* the *Carolina Quarterly,* the *Centennial
Review,* the *Chariton Review,* the *Christian Science Monitor,* the *Comstock Review,
Confrontation,* the *Connecticut River Review, cream city review,* the *Evansville
Review,* the *Flint Hills Review,* the *Florida Review, Flyway, Fugue, Gulf Coast,
Hayden's Ferry Review,* the *Indiana Review, The Journal, Kalliope, Kestrel, The Ledge,
Louisiana Literature,* the *MacGuffin,* the *Mississippi Review,* the *Nebraska Review,*
the *New Delta Review, New Letters, Nightsun, Nimrod,* the *Paterson Literary
Review, Pleiades, Poems and Plays, Poet Lore, Poets On, Prairie Schooner, Puerto
del Sol, Quarter after Eight, Quarterly West,* the *Red Rock Review, Shenandoah,
So to Speak,* the *South Carolina Review,* the *Southern Poetry Review, The Southern
Review, Sundog: The Southeast Review, Tampa Review,* the *Texas Review, Thin Air
Magazine,* the *Vanderbilt Review, Whiskey Island Magazine,* the *Wisconsin Review*
and the *Yale Angler Journal.*

For my grandchildren,

Eric Raymond Jokl

Nicholas Charles Jokl

Samuel Shipley Jokl

Hazel Rose Jokl

Isabella Anna Jokl

Other Books by Vivian Shipley

Poems out of Harlan County (1989)
Devil's Lane (1996)
Crazy Quilt (1999)
Fair Haven (2000)
When There Is No Shore (2002)
Gleanings: Old Poems, New Poems (2003)
Hardboot: Poems New & Old (2005)
All of Your Messages Have Been Erased (2010)

Chapbooks

Jack Tales (1982)
How Many Stones? (1998)
Echo & Anger, Still (1999)
Down of Hawk (2001)
Fishing Poems (2001)
Greatest Hits: 1974-2010 (2011)

CONTENTS

I

THE POET AS IMPOSTER

I'm a dominatrix with a weakness for games
that require memory and feel. Poems or contests
with absolutes don't exhilarate me like anarchistic
skirmishes. Actually, I like the duel between good
and evil combined with a challenge that is
altogether tactile. Zesting is one of my favorite

exercises because every lemon, like every poem,
is different. I am also a fool for smell. I get off
on knowing I have a powerful, secret ingredient:
lemon rind packed with oil can change even
the odor of my dungeon. The pith, or albedo,
is dense with pectin bitter enough to wreak havoc

on almost any dish, on any client. Only a hand trained
by a pen knows the exact force needed to tease apart
the mesh of pleasure and pain, how to lift golden peel
from bitter dross. I have no need for chains, cuffs,
collars, boxes. There's a perfect tool for zesting—
one that sports a curved blade. Satisfying as a whip,

there are small indentations on its handle for thumb
and forefinger. The lemon, like a head ready
to be scalped, rests in the palm of my left hand
while my right grasps the peeler and negotiates
between rind and the spongy part beneath. Used
with proper pressure, it produces perfect little

strips of skin that curl through five beveled holes
at its tip. It's not enough for a poet or for a mistress
to control just the body, it is the mind I am after.
Comforting to a man or woman like sucking on a bottle
while wearing a cloth diaper, simple but exacting,
the act of zesting can engender a Zen state of being.

In the Hammer Throw
Ring with the Poet

Tyrannosaurus Rex trapezoids,
thighs and rear, I am spinning.
Earth is spiraling; I want to keep

doing this. Cosmic. Interplanetary.
Zen. I am Mercury. I am Venus.
No, I am Harold Connolly, ribboned

in Olympic gold from Melbourne, 1956,
ballet slippers designed by my Irish mother,
a vaudeville dancer. Confined to a seven

foot wide concrete circle, not fourteen
lines of a sonnet, I pirouette, whirl, lance
the hammer maybe three stories high,

a football field long, then the yelp. If only I'd
overcome gravity like negativity, my hammer
would never touch ground. The secret

is the pendulum, the system: centrifugal force
created when I begin to rotate and speed up
to sixty miles per hour, gripping a four foot

wire attached to sixteen pounds of hammer.
Twirl four times, no prodigy, I can't get
away with three, I lean back, sit in space.

Arms are stretched straight out because,
to borrow from physics, the longer the lever,
the farther the throw. For me, it's *kamiwaza,*

Japanese for super human feat, or divine
intervention when words flow in a single
eruption like 8 mm film spooling on tile floor.

I have been known to crutch through a poem,
but centered, brute strength or no, I can't
muscle the hammer forward. Like fingers

probing my spine to rotate me through the tango,
it is a guide, tries to show me how to avoid being
banished from festival fields because weight

of my subjects pock lawns manicured like Japanese
tankas and rengas. My hammer in hand, I am
a leaf shedding a globule of rain that quick silvers

a glissando all down the center vein. Like a spring
willow, the green, tip unbends. My heart and
my hammer are one. Transcendent. Then the thud.

Why the Poet Plays Jacks

Knowing every trick, a gladiator
in the ring, I'm the first to call out:

no overs, splits, jack-in-the-box.
As jacks age, the nubs wear down,

so I carry my own set in a velvet bag
strapped to my waist. They're lighter

on fingertips that I have hardened
by sweeping dust into a pan. Getting

jiggy with the rhythm, *eggs in the basket,*
double bounce, and *over the moon,*

I never throw the four headed pins
too far apart. Toss the ball high enough,

I can pick up eight, maybe ten before it
bounces. To be ready for the unexpected,

the crazy ricochet off an edge, I stay away
from table tops and linoleum floors, train

on uneven ground, maybe a flagstone walk
with concrete missing. To be a winner,

I practice with morning sun in my eye.
In competition, all poets face the light.

FOR THE RECORD,
THE POET BLOWS BUBBLES

Even after limbering up my lips at open mic,
I'm nervous going for the record of *largest
unassisted bubble* in *Guinness World Records.*
I chew, smack, pucker up, and puff, then blow

a 19 ¾ inch bubble I keep inflated for 4.9 seconds.
Gum masking my cheeks and chin, I am good
but not good enough to beat the champ: 20 inches,
5 seconds set by Chad Fell in Alabama April, 2004.

Discouraged, I think of a fire balloon I released
after I'd set off all my 4th of July fireworks. Easing it
from a cardboard box, I lifted paper, frail as gossamer
or a ghost. Red, white and blue tissue waited for me

to breathe life into walls and set it adrift. Igniting
the basket of straw dangling beneath, hot air rising,
when the balloon whispered *enough,* I gave it up
to midnight sky watching for ten minutes or more

until it became a star like I was determined to be.
For months on end, flossing regularly and careful
never to swallow, I chomp then masticate through
3 bags of Double Bubble a week. Per contest rules,

I tear into 3 pieces of gum, measure my bubble
horizontally with calipers. Picture me with the jaws
of a poet chewing a full 17 minutes before I add
breath to cut down sugar, not because it may crystalize

to Hallmark rhyme, but because it limits size, decreases
elasticity necessary for resilience and flexibility.
The secret of champions is in taste, knowing when to
blow; totally sugar-free gum won't expand, let me hold

a bubble aloft willing the air not to break through like I might do if I accept a cousin's double dog dare and skate on first ice or inject sentiment into my poem. Sweetness is a bubble gum competitor's worst enemy—a poet's too.

The Poet as Surfer Chick

The combo of combat-oriented martial arts
and hot yoga can still get me stoked to spill out
poems the way I did catching a wave in one deep

stroke, making it look like the surf came to me.
1960s, Southern California, Surfing Safari. I wore
a string bikini, puka shells, timed my tanning

like a Perdue roaster on a spit, used lemon juice
to sun bleach my hair. No aerial maneuvers, by day,
I rode a longboard. Dude, I was a surfer chick.

A reef, forgiving as a friend in workshop, softened
minor wipe outs, the 2 and 3 foot ones—glassy,
breaking small. Even when there was a big hump

up, grinding, boils-up-the-sand bone crusher,
I rode the curl, learned to work with the talent
I was dealt. Now, I'd like to say to these young

bodies here with me at Bread Loaf that I was
throwing heat before they were born, show what
an old-school switchfoot can do. If this were surfer

camp and not a writing retreat, I'd be on my back,
stuffing myself like a sausage into a wet suit,
ready to split, to slice the long blue tube. Early on,

I learned to turn upside down like a snapping turtle
with my board or hardback if I was about to be
hammered—waves or words, *keep your day job,*

both slap and sting. One smart babe, I'd perfected
standing on a board or at a podium in a long low
crouch, legs spread, my rump in the air—an angry

stink bug will give you the picture. Butt boot camp
gave me strong quads I needed to keep knees bent,
back hunched, ready to flip the bird to rip outs or

thank you for sending. But hey, the best thing about
surfing was that I didn't have to think, only paddle
even when a wave broke leaving me on blank shore.

Surf-a-Rama or Sunken Garden, I'm a surfer chick—
though for the sake of visual and verbal accuracy,
I might be labeled *Hen.* Whatever. No worries, man.

Rules for the Poet When Swimming with Sharks

1.   If a hammerhead or a great white makes waves
during your workshop or poetry reading, don't flap
your elbows or slap at it with rolled manuscripts.

2.   Sharks thrive on visual stimulation. Blow out
candles. Ease away from the podium. Wait
ten minutes before going for a light switch. Join
hands to keep karma with other poets. It's okay
to recite poems memorized in fifth grade,
even Kilmer, in desperation, Longfellow.

3.   Rule of thumb: it's a shark not a dolphin if it is
slamming about a room, hugging, blowing
air kisses. Performers, sharks are almost
all instinct and no brain. No sense of occasion,
they'll crash any gig, underwater or not.

4.   Being eyed by a shark can be exasperating. Don't
rush or shift from foot to foot to induce motion
sickness. Sharks are immune. They are, however,
dyslexic. Flash cover quotes and prize winning
poems directly in front of both eyes. Better yet,
stop reading! Pull your new hardback from
a knapsack. When the shark noses you, hit it
directly on the snout with repeated hard jabs.

5.   Sharks have short attention spans, leave if there is
no open mic. If all else fails, sharks have a keen sense
of hearing. Sing *The Battle Hymn of the Republic* at
the top of your lungs then swing into another verse:
Glory, Glory, Halleluiah! His truth is marching on.

THE POET AS HAG MOTH

No strength or ferocity to protect myself
against being eaten alive by mice, shrews,

or poets masquerading as robins and canaries,
garter snakes, weasels, even foxes, can snap me

up in a second. A witness protection program
is what I need, to live in disguise like a hag moth

caterpillar. Irritating spines for protection,
so ugly nobody would give me a second look,

on a car hood or behind a podium, I'll appear
rough, a piece of bark unless a hand brushes

me off and its brain registers: soft flesh. At first,
workshop drama queen, decked out as a dark

brown larva, eight long meaty appendages will
cover my back with a backward twist like

dreadlocks or a disheveled wig. In fact, they
are muscular hooks covered with feathery black

stinging hairs. Two rows of soft suckers for legs
will provide the illusion of being a push-over

while I sniff up and notebook images, titles, but
avoid clichés from other poets. Grown, a female

during the day, to blend in, I will fly on cocoa
colored wings. A balloon for an abdomen,

my hind legs sprouting brilliant yellow tufts,
anyone would swear I am carrying honey, pollen

sweet, intense as a haiku. If I stay camouflaged
as a bee, even in apple blossom metaphors, I might

be ignored during class commentary. Predators
are too smart to mess with stingers. Switch hitting,

a male hag moth by night, I poetry slam at Bar 13,
Courting Risk, Accentos, then bomb at The Shrine

and Inspired Word. Not like the other poets flitting
around with their flat scales shimmering in shades

of Indian silk, my verse like my wings will be clear,
my body, wasp shaped. No one is interested in a wasp.

No Gold Lamé for the Poet

1. The Poet Thinks about Christo, about Thirdness

Just about every day, I think about thirdness: Christo
draping Berlin's Reichstag in a million square feet
of aluminum fabric, swathing Paris' Pont Neuf
in 454,178 square feet of champagne polyamide
that shimmered like silk. I think about veils: Christo
in a park in Basel, Switzerland, bagging 161 trees
in black and white polyester mesh. When the sun
was behind the trees, every branch, every leaf was
visible, but shielded from light, corrosion, fading
and leaching. Curing country ham in our farm's
smoke house, my father taught me meat rubbed
in salt, laced with red and black pepper, shrouded
in muslin didn't spoil in air. However, I am not
about to be Julia Child, wrapping Caribbean fish
in banana leaves to protect it from tongued flames.
I do debate whether to veil poetry with abstraction
or lift black mesh from a widow's face, white
netting before a bride's first kiss. Balking at
wrapping gold lamé around my head to scarf
a scar half-mooning my scalp after a brain tumor
was removed, I do wonder when the Bronx Zoo's
guard turns his head, if I should shatter glass
over the Burmese python balled over the walkway
in a hollow log. Rubbing brown, then yellow,
I could break the sheen of what lies beneath
Salome's seventh veil, of what cannot be contained.

2. The Poet Thinks about Boxes

I make time to think a lot about boxes: sizes,
shapes, materials, stackability, cost. I think about
waxed, unwaxed, corrugated cardboard, shippers,
wired wooden sides, those with pressboard ends,

paper-covered slats, the depth, width and solidness
of the bottom. I even have a moral order of boxes:
perfect boxes, good boxes, bad boxes and totally useless
boxes. There are active boxes, inhaling and exhaling
like tidal pools at Morgan Point. Inactive boxes
cornered in the shed let me finger rough surfaces
of my past, my grandmother's purgatory: Limoges,
Staffordshire, Dresden too chipped to display,
too good to trash. The walls of a box can shelter,
but also disturb equilibrium of, say, apples. Crated,
Macintosh, Macouns, don't spill to rot, to blossom,
to pollinate. I can't hold a box up to light to make
the interior visible even if a perfect box says, *Trespass*.
Why is it I oscillate between statement and suggestion
in poems that like boxes make me question whether
to uncrate anxiety over my glaucoma, or erect
a screen of ambiguity about a poet's loss of vision?

3. The Poet Thinks about Birthdays

I should be against ideas that come in containers,
but I think all of the time about robin egg blue boxes
topped with white satin. Who among us isn't a fool
for a surprise when packages are nicely wrapped and
tied? Rodin first sculpted Balzac naked, but I suppose,
like a lover, he became jealous. Taking a cape, Rodin
soaked it in wet plaster and draped Balzac's figure—
the body was after all only a crate for the magic,
for *Le Père Goriot*. Six years old, it was not the thought
but the gift that counted for me. I didn't want barriers,
pauses, paper to rip, just pile upon pile of presents
circling me, end to end, covered wagons pulled around
the campfire. At seventy, I still don't have the time
to read cards, wait for the song, poke ribbons in paper
plates, a birthday bouquet. Yes, I know Aristotle said
in *Rhetoric* that metaphor is the token of genius, but
I don't have an eye for resemblances, do not want
metaphor as tissue, a lid to lift. Anticipation, hope, lead
me to disappointment. So, I keep tugging until the inside

is revealed. No predictability in life, I don't cast about
for drama, have no need to be provoked by a box circled
with gold foil ribbon Martha Stewart has scissored to curls.

4. The Poet Thinks about Sonnets

I think, although less often, about sonnets: Petrarchan,
Spenserian, Shakespearean. I debate: quatrain/couplet
or octave/sestet, leap of logic or steady steps to epiphany?
I have no moral order for poems. Villanelles are road
maps I hope lead me somewhere. A sestina's six six-line
stanzas march to the final envoy that I always do first.
Like an AAA destination, it maps my trip. I can goad
nouns, verbs, adjectives and adverbs into equality but
cannot decide which ones should be kept trousered
or buttoned. Never into nuance, silence, subtlety,
or mustering the inexplicable, I do seek rough edges,
nubby, wooly, deckled rims. Isaac Newton reincarnated,
with no stanza pattern as velvet cushion, I like line
breaks that push words off balance into white space,
a force like universal gravity. Reassured as I now am
by a beginning, middle and end, pattern helps me, but
does not break up binary thinking. Afraid to use banisters
as parallel bars to swing down three steps at a time,
way too old to trot up Emily Dickinson's *stairway
of surprise*, I may need to depend on rails and rhyme,
count steps like syllables—safe with iambic pentameter.

MARK MCGWIRE, NOT THE POET, BREAKS BABE RUTH'S RECORD

I inhale all air I have ever taken, exhale August.
My bat, a magnet for the ball, I can see the seams.
Heliumed into a balloon of the girl I might have been,

crowds are a neck arched as I tag base after base.
No, no high fives for me, no medals ever dripped
off of my breasts. But I knew about first base,

second base, third base, and girls who held the record
for home runs, whispered names of boys who scored
them. Covington, Kentucky. 1975. I was a real pro

at distracting backseat hands: the Big Red Machine.
I quoted stats, not poems: Cincinnati won 108 games,
beat Boston Red Sox in 7 games in the World Series.

Reds hit 124 home runs, stole 168 bases. Pete Rose,
career hit leader, batted .317 with 112 runs scored.
The two-time most valuable player, Joe Morgan,

batted .327, and he had 17 home runs with 94 r.b.i.
The only gloves I wore were white ones I could
strip to show off my hot pink nails when I gave

out MVP trophies at Little League. No sweat, but
my legs were still like dried petals, half curled, calves
tight and thighs tense. Still conscious of their size,

I will not breathe on the hall mirror to finger my profile,
or outline what I could have been. I see the woman
I am, pulling hair back to tighten skin around my eyes.

STRIKE THREE
AND THE POET'S OUT

Trained to sit in parks, amnesia of sun,
sweat under my breasts because
he sucked them, I can't pitch a baseball
low, outside, curve, sinker, hook or right
down the middle. No Alex Rodriguez,
Sammy Sosa, I'm also not Babe Ruth's
daughter, didn't give birth to a grandson
creating another Sultan of Swat.

As Eric swings and swings and swings,
I blame myself and so does he. Why should
a poet know that the batter tugs his cap
while a catcher reverses his, or that pitchers
rub new balls and a base stealer balances
like a traffic cop with white gloves pointing
opposite ways. I answer my son with
a question Walt Whitman asked Tom Harned:
The fellow who pitches the ball aims to pitch
it in such a way the batter cannot hit it?

No underhanded pitches on this field,
I tell Eric, no softball. Obvious moves
like pawing the dirt with your foot or lifting
your leg, knee bent, send a telegraph
to home plate. Spit on the ground; appear
confused, afraid, just up from the minors;
have a face that couldn't tell a lie. Your arm
should flirt, keeping men on base off balance
by never hitting the mitt the runner sees
you aim for. Let the ball float, a kite,
the string invisible to the batter who will
learn the wild pitch is winged deadeye,
is too swift for detection and final.

How the Poet Learns to Rebound

Knocked down, I elbowed back under the rim,
ready like Bill Russell to rebound fifty times or more
to stay in the game. Splay-legged as Dennis Rodman,
I had learned from rejection slips that I had to grab
with both hands, cannonball a pass. Blocking
anyone who tried to whip the ball off my head, trip

me like a mark, half court, I swiveled, keeping other
hot shots off balance. Hitting that turnaround J,
token pressure, I got in the other guy's shirt to tip
the ball to myself. Taught to echo Stevens, Eliot,
even Frost, I mimicked Scottie Pippen's quick release
jumper in the lane, Ron Harper's downtown heaves,

and the slo-mo pick-and-roll of John Stockton
and Karl Malone. I could never heave hard enough
to break through glass, but I was a hit at slams with
bellowing breaths like Willis Reed at the foul line.
If Bill Russell hadn't been on the Celts' bench
resting after wind-mill hooks, he would've cackled

jai alai garbage time. I had sense enough not to try
imitating Michael Jordan's fall-away shot in the lane,
tongue-dangling drive to the hoop or ass-wagging
back-to-the-basket pivot. Booed off Dodge's stage,
I lived through Luc Longley's Keatonesque pratfall,
but why go there? No Hardaway, but a Kentucky

hardboot, I never walked the ball up slow as a mule;
I took guff dished out by critics, coaches like Rupp.
Even so, I'll never end my career as Michael Jordan
did with a move like Keats' *Ode on a Grecian Urn,*
winning his sixth N.B.A. title, causing his defender
to stumble, mystified: *What men or gods are these?*

THE POET AS BUSTER KEATON
IN *HARD LUCK*

It's a dark night in a nameless town; you're a nameless
    man. You see a pair of headlights approaching, you take
    four quick steps into the road, go to a half crouch
with both hands resting on your knees, eyes squeezed tight

as if you are about to sneeze. Two beams hurtle toward
    you, dividing into motorcycles. You open your eyes,
    straighten up and walk off of the road. You have
not been run over. Swallow a bottle of poison, it will be

bootleg gin; lie in front of a train, it will never reach you.
    Try again. Walk off that movie onto *Sherlock Jr's* set.
    Dream yourself into yet another film: stroll down
the middle aisle of Loew's theater, hop up, then pierce

the screen, and fight to keep up with the action as you
    do playing hero in *The Three Ages*. Flee the police
    station, run up a fire escape to the roof, leap
toward the next-door building, pass the parapet, drop

three stories. A human cannon ball ripping canvas
    awnings, catch a drainpipe that will swing around
    a hundred and eighty degrees, rifling you through
an open window straight into a pole. Slide down.

Come to rest on the ladder of a fire engine which wails
    you back to the police station where you started.
    That's your problem: like a poet, you want something
to happen; nothing keeps happening, but in a big way.

BOOTLEGGER: THE POET
AS NELLIE GREEN

Behind my back, people call me Tugboat Annie,
but none dare say it to my face. Talmadge Hotel,

my speakeasy on the Farm River in East Haven,
Connecticut, was a stagecoach repair shop operated

by my father, Charlie Green. He brewed hootch,
mountain dew, white lightning, pop-skull, rot gut,

what my hillbilly uncle called Kentucky-mule.
Letting me kick the barrel for aging, Uncle Lanny

taught me to swing a jug from my index finger
and old-timey songs like *The Kentucky Moonshiner*:

I've been a moonshiner goin' on seventeen year.
I spent all my money on whiskey and beer.
I'll go to some holler and set up my still,
And sell you a gallon for a two-dollar bill.

Far from Appalachian hollers, and more practical,
Daddy showed me nooks in the cellar where I

could stash oak casks and gallon bottles of booze
from New York City. In the Roaring Twenties,

I was the fastest rumrunner along the East Coast.
Feds, cops, nobody could catch me or my chief pilot,

"Wing" St. Clair. Out-racing Coast Guard he'd shout
Here's mud in your eye across Long Island Sound.

Safe in my boats, the Sparkle, Betty T and a converted
subchaser I christened Uno, none of my crew needed

to pack a gun. Tipped off about a raid by the sheriff,
a good customer, we stuck bottles of moonshine

in a field of cow manure. A real scorcher the day
feds searched, July heat caused bottles to blow up

and spout like humpback whales about to breach.
The jugs were up, the jig was up, but no one wanted

to wade that field to find out for sure. In my spare
time a poet, but never one who confessed all after

a few rounds, I took that explosion to heart. 1933,
Prohibition ended, I used my experience distilling

spirits as a way to counsel steady customers
in my new nightspot, Nellie Green's. Sampling

bourbon, vodka, gin, Scottish malts I'd imported,
we explored a variant of the uncertainty principle:

the more research we drank, the less reliable
the results. Teaching regulars impurity is what gives

whiskey its flavor, I urged the likes of Rudy Valee,
John Barrymore, Tyrone Power, Bing Crosby,

and Jack London to pour out their hearts, memories
they'd suppressed. Act out, or belt out, lyrics, stories

and poems revealing warts and all, or fermenting,
repressed emotion would erupt as temperatures rose.

Drinking Moonshine, the Poet Ties One on

Walking back from services in the sweat of evening, Mother
and I stopped to be civil. Just sitting, Uncle Alvey possessed

his porch, dog. I felt metal in his leg, a war wound, making
sure my birth paid for *pain of woman* mother used as whip

to make me behave. Past the age to admit fingers tightened
her glove, I stood while she told everyone I wrote poetry,

was bound for Lexington that fall. Our preacher warned me
about strong drink, shouting: *train, beerbelly, hands puzzling*

the body. I had learned from cousins to pay him no mind.
Deciding to sin a little, I found barrels and copper sheeting

out by the corner shed. Drinking from a still with condensers
made of automobile radiators that left lead salts was deadly

as selling to strangers. I had heard Uncle Lanny's prohibition
stories about neighbors who'd drawn big claims, sometimes

up to fifty dollars, to witness against a friend. Hard times,
people needed cash. Government set relatives on each other.

Trusting my father to have sense enough not to use soldered
joints, that I wouldn't be blinded, I drank. Climbing a man's

world, Jack, flinging red and tan beans, I got higher, higher,
putting miles between me and women smothering in oilcloth.

Another drink, one more, I was sitting with men on a bench
in Alexander's grocery: crock, bare floors, charred coffeepot.

Fried ham from fingers holding smell of livestock, there was
enough for feasting but nothing left over to clean, store for

breakfast. No ceremony, no grace, sleeves to wipe gravy,
one plate to clean, no women to keep me from men, real life

lived out of doors. No Kentucky rain. It's Connecticut.
Leaning up against the bar at Rudy's, I don't have to hide

behind lattice work under the back porch. I drink Jim Beam.
Marty fills my glass: shot; beer; shot; beer. Again, I dip into

white lightning. Rust freckled tin cup drains to hooked rugs,
Clabber Girl barns, I have tried to hide under a crazy quilt.

On the Inca Trail with the Poet

Girl, We Couldn't Get Much Higher
— Jim Morrison

Obsolete as a Underwood ribbon of black unspooling,
I do not want my story to be the dew that almost frosted,
the moon that was almost full. I know how to live
by the sun, not the clock, have witnessed mountains
of Harlan County open into an ocean of fog, but I haven't
seen Peru, the Andes that spill out of *The Sophisticated
Traveler* in *The New York Times*. A poet, I'm open

to what they might teach me, coming hard and swift
like the grace of love. After losing my way in middle age,
cocoa leaves might help me remember why it was
I used to want a song to go on forever, *Love Me Tender*
looping on a reel to *Heartbreak Hotel*. Machu Picchu.
I will hold the name in my mouth like a tooth no one
can extract. Trekking the Inca Trail to this city ringed

with mountains that Spanish conquistadors somehow
overlooked, my heart might open to new desire rising
with swiftness of dawn, stay awake through dusk. Hiking
six to eight hours a day at altitudes of over 10,000 feet,
my knees will migrate as geese do while I glide like
Georgetown's crew misting the Potomac River. Round
shouldered with age, the Appalachians already had

a hold on me. Furrowing ridges, stones and roots troubled
my grandfather's plow, turned rows into a scribble
punctuated with limestone, feldspar, deep tubers of oak
felled long ago. *Put your back into it*, he'd tell me, *Take
a hold and pull.* I did. Still my past was not quenching as
water can be. Moonlit cedar, birch set against winter sky,
rumble of train or lingering echo of whistles didn't suck me

to ecstasy, pop my body from its socket. No Carole King,
I'd felt no quiver of a high board, put no kickers in back

of my pickup. Now sagging like an unpainted cabin on stilts
at the foot of a hollow, I have a chance to out-distance
Pablo Neruda: *Then up the ladder of the earth I climbed /
through the barbed jungle's thickets / until I reached you
Machu Picchu.* With eighty pounds strapped on their backs,

wearing shoes named Yankees made from old tires,
porters glide as if they were Peggy Fleming. I check
for skates. Following the Urubamba River, climbing
to 800 feet, my feet slalom. I never thought I'd end up
too old, always thought I could strip to spandex and jog
five miles on asphalt. My backpack, weighted with journals
filled with memories I can't shed, strains my abdomen. No

sinewed rhomboids and trapezoids, there is no difference
between how I feel and how I look. Fear, but no adrenaline,
someone must have nailed my boots to the ground. I hear
my grandmother repeat, *There is no rest for the wicked,*
as we set up camp on agricultural terraces of Llactapata,
an Inca outpost. My heart in epilogue, I wake from night
to plunge into day, an endless rosary of pain I finger

each of the 4,000 feet I climb all the way from the river.
Our destination spells my future: Warmiwañusca,
Dead Woman's Pass. Wherever I go, my thighs, calves
come with me. I chew cocoa leaves, stuff a wad big
as a knot of chewing tobacco into my mouth and push
it to the side with my tongue like Uncle Justus taught me
when I turned thirteen. I try everything, leave one foot

in place before pushing off with the other. Too tired
to slow down, keep a rhythm, breathe through my nose,
out through my mouth, oxygenate, I can only pant.
Each step is the last I will take. Should I push off with
my left or my right foot is the biggest decision I will ever
make. Reaching Warmiwañusca Pass at 13,780 feet, I'm the
oldest woman at the highest point on the Inca Trail.

THE POET HIKES UP
AV. DU PÈRE-LACHAISE

Smashed into francs, pounded into dirt, beer bottle
    caps carpet the space framing Jim Morrison's
grave. Yes, it's Paris, but it's not Dom Perignon;
    it's a keg party, another chance to chant *Toga,*
Toga, echo the Doors' *C'mon baby light my fire*

that lures me. That, and the right to brag I fit
    into my old jeans embroidered with daisies
around the crotch, razored to look ripped out
    at the knees. Riding a Harley with James Dean,
I would never have squealed or begged to slow

down. Goading him to fly close to trees, guard rails,
    my feet tucked well away from burns and exhaust,
I'd ask my *Rebel without a Cause* to shimmy back
    and fill space between my thighs so I could
forget where my body ended and his began. Barreling

out, *Freedom's just another word for nothing left to lose,*
    I still can do Janis Joplin, hang out, play acoustic.
No sod covers Jim Morrison's coffin, just soil mixed
    with fine gravel, a plastic red rose, a note from Stan.
Rectangular and flat, the stone is not original, is replaced

at least once a month whenever it's covered in graffiti:
    We love you, Jim from Edwin H. and Emile C.
Beneath a peace sign cut in the O in JAMES DOUGLAS,
    1940-1971, it's enough for me that there is space for
two lines from a poem where they will last, for a while.

 **II**

THE POET

While waiting for a blizzard, I buy
more salt and sand, an extra shovel,
a gallon of milk, gas both cars up.
You get the picture. I'm a safety pin,
belt, and suspenders type. School is
cancelled, so are planes. Marooned,
a time out, some write love poems,
but not me. Sleet changes to rain
and I can't enjoy rivers overflowing
from gutters filled with leaves. Snow
does not fall. Instead, robins come,
hundreds of them eating red berries
from my holly tree. No weathermen,
their red breasts forecast: spring. So,
why don't I double stock picnic baskets,
buy extra shears to cut tulips, daffodils?

No Crown for the Poet

Holding two six packs of Schlitz, the man standing
next to me in line at Kroger's is laughing up a storm
as his wife holds the *Star* pointing first at me, then
my picture which is right above headlines of a story
about a woman arrested for soliciting in mid-town

Manhattan. I'd never been to New York City, but I
grabbed the *Star* knocking over a box of Life Savers
and stacks of Mr. Goodbars. The Associated Press
headlines above my picture blared: *Imposter Wears
Crown; Homecoming Queen Sobs!* Imagine how I felt.

There wasn't a line about me in *National Enquirer*.
Newspaper clippings I'd gotten from every state
in the union were carefully trimmed and mounted
to fill a scrapbook. I even saved the letter from
an eighty year old man out in Oklahoma who wanted

to come all the way to Kentucky and save me. Naturally,
he figured only a fallen woman could have such a thing
happen to her right in the middle of 50,000 people.
I sure hadn't done anything to deserve what didn't take
place that October afternoon, but I resolved to sin as fast

as possible in the future. I stopped attending worship
at Methodist Youth Fellowship, began writing poems
filled with desire for revenge. No more nice girl!
I wouldn't give back my crown to the Kitten Club,
sponsors of the event. Winning that contest had been

serious business; my Kappa Delta sisters must have
hung at least two hundred posters around UK's campus
and believe me, it was no picnic finding a suit in just
the right Kentucky wildcat blue. Our pledges handed
out leaflets in the CU at noon, tied balloons stenciled

with *Victory for Vivian* on car antennas, passed out
Dum-Dum's in the library wearing tee-shirts that said,
We're Suckers for Shipley. My rival finally struck back,
plastering flyers over all of the campus windows saying,
Shipley Sucks. I for one wouldn't stoop to dirty tactics,

but I did try to get her arrested for defacing state property.
At the University of Kentucky, basketball brought in big
money and Adolph Rupp liked to keep his star players happy.
My campaign manager hadn't counted on Cotton Nash's
girlfriend getting elected to Homecoming Court. Julie was

crowned. I cried. Cotton beamed and my escort shouted,
You've crowned the wrong girl! Open the album. It's on the
piano. Trophy clutched, roses hanging at my side like a hand
broken from its wrist, the first picture is me with my mouth
twisted, standing on the fifty-yard line just off the field.

It was right after the half time when President Donovan
himself came to correct the gross injustice. I tinted that photo
from the *Star* and enlarged my face. As paint aged, it became
opaque. Original lines haunt the portrait, a specter: 1960's
hair, blooming; eyes and my smile fixed as if hooked onto

my ears. Forty years later, I can say anything. I might
go to a therapist who'd help me recall the Athletic Director
switching the names so the announcer would crown
the wrong girl. Maybe that happened, maybe it didn't.
Rupp's innocence can't be proved. He's dead; there wasn't

a chapter about me in his biography. The orders could have
been given by University Public Relations to attract press to
Lexington. I might unearth Senator McCarthy, have him start
an investigation, or have the FBI find if there was a plot
to undermine democracy by ignoring student votes, the voice

of the American people. I suppose it's just possible that
Communists had infiltrated the election, figuring they'd
practice first on a Homecoming Queen, then move onto

the White House. Not letting go of that Saturday afternoon
is as productive as speculating on afterlife. If I stepped

back onto that field, I'd still be whimpering to reporters,
I feel like a clod! or agreeing with the Student Council's
leader that the word *queen* must have been misplaced like
an unframed photograph, never asking why the runner-up
was given my crown. Anyway, I would have run even if I'd

known the consequences. It would have been a shame to miss
all those headlines. Now, I want to turn, go up to myself
at twenty and shout: *Grab the roses, flash the bird! Sprint the stadium.*
Rip poems you had stuffed into your bra, shred Marilyn Monroe's
breasts, fling them on the turf like a wildcat to confetti your own parade.

THE POET'S LUCKY NUMBER

Rocking on the front porch with eyes closed to feel
late sun, my grandmother preached to her congregation
of chickens and cats, *The hairs of your head are numbered.*
As a barber shaved my head with an electric razor,

I pictured her hands, fingers layered between knuckles,
and thumbs twiddling like blades of a reel mower
cutting hay. Piling around me like stacks of wheat
in Brueghel's *The Harvesters* before it is gathered

and tied, my hair was red then gold in the air as it
dropped. *Way too pretty to throw away*, the orderly said
as he gathered it in a sack for me to keep. The night
before the meningioma was removed, I had to translate

the medical word for *brain tumor* to my family while they
circled around me. Holding hands as they sang *Amazing
Grace,* their trust was in the mighty fortress of God, not
the surgeon. Folding my fingers into my palms, index

and thumbs pointed to heaven, I used to play *Here's
the church, here's the steeple. Open the doors and here's the people.*
Before the operation, my hands were strapped down.
I couldn't pray without them. My number was not up.

I could add. Emptying a bag I brought from the hospital,
I counted each strand of hair, told myself: *Hustle! Ink
your lucky number on a forearm, go to Lighthouse Deli,
buy a fistful of Quik Pic, Lotto, Play Four and Power Ball.*

BE *WHOLE:* THE POET'S PRAYER

I hold my breath as the ultrasound lines shape of skull,
thumbs, and fingers like germinating beans. Lungs

not yet inflated, ribs thin as twigs. The aorta. I name
arms, legs, spine of Matthew, the third boy to be stuffed

under my heart. I have a bad memory, can't recall giving
birth to my second son, Todd. I was pregnant but

with a growth that did not blossom as he did. A tumor
in my brain didn't part my hair or sprout from the bulb,

bigger than an amaryllis, hidden above my right eye.
Like a tomb, bone does not swell. Early in the morning,

seizures jerked me as if I were a puppet on strings. Todd
had to tear his way out of me into his first afternoon,

and turn for milk, for life, to the hands of a stranger who
fingered his cheek. No way to scalpel the heart, his cry

stayed inside me to fill my breasts that were left to burn,
unplucked as live oak leaves that hang on to be tormented

by winter wind. Even if he could have sucked my nipples,
Todd's body would not have shielded me from arteriogram,

femoral stick done from a textbook diagram. The technician
did not know I wrote poetry, who was being entered or if

a clot might break loose. Smell was not my baby's mouth,
but sour stabs of the surgeon's breath as he pulled down

his green mask to tell me the news was good—only half
of my skull would be replaced, and the meningioma

could be removed. Vain as ever, I knew hair grows back,
even on heads of the dead. A faucet of anesthesia dripped;

I held my doctor's wrist as if asking him to go with me
to the confrontation of something. A hospital sheet

was not eased over my eyes; breath of desire returned.
Today, a nurse pins up a Polaroid of Matthew burrowing

in my womb. Like weathermen, new doctors have posted
my delivery chart with alerts, given me storm warnings.

The tumor's souvenir, my fingers have stiffened as if from
deep cold and I can't stitch an heirloom quilt for him. If I

don't live to hold my third son, Matthew will have my poem,
my love he can wrap around himself or hold up as a flare.

CHRIST AND SKATERBUGS WALK ON WATER, BUT NOT THE POET

Visualize your villanelle. Next, *Analyze your repeating lines.*
Bugeja's advice in *The Art and Craft of Poetry* is useless.

My mother's questions about my son are effective, arouse
guilt, work like a burglar sneaking past North Haven's

librarian to bag reading room silence. No sense of the rhyme
words, it's hands that repeat, Todd's hands gripping my leg

as I try to ease the car door shut. Coated with the flour from
a canister he'd pulled over his head, my son's face whiteouts

lines on pages that stiffen like percale I draped over crib bars
as I tried to trick him into napping. An umbilical cord still

binds my wrists, and I cannot count five tercets, a quatrain,
repeat the first and third line alternately on fingers indented

with a Braille alphabet lettered by Todd's teeth. Weekday
mornings disintegrate: I go home, a babysitter leaves, whole

afternoons fray and I figure out why soldiers stood beneath
the cross casting lots for Christ's cloak. There were no seams

to unravel. To do revisions, I blanket bedroom windows
to prolong sleep, but a picture develops—two-year-old hands

with crocus: heads stunned, yellow as jaundice. Evergreen
suit trimmed with red braid, Todd melted his spot in March

snow that claimed outside toys. New, his words stiffened as
if salted by breath. Rail straight, their edges were snowdrops

resurrecting frozen ground that I had troweled in October.
Masquerading as Shelley, I touched each bloom to teach him

faith, that spring would come and about planting with double
nosed bulbs that played hide and seek with winter. Spearing

matted oak leaves, tulips were opening to tongues of flame
I'll never have. Either in mourning for villanelles I didn't

write, or teaching Todd to speak, I repeated once then twice,
my voice ascending to a crescendo: *Flow-er, Flow-er, Flow-er.*

What the Poet Learns
about the Letter Z

Start with A for alligator. B, C and D will blossom
and ripen. At four, a child not ready to read alone, Todd
fingers each shape. Until he no longer needs me to translate,

I could tell him anything; for no good reason, I might say
Q is R and M could be W if only he would walk on hands
or hold his book upside down. In this first flourishing

of interest, I overdo it, explaining what each day was like
for my mother as a girl growing up on a farm near Somerset,
Kentucky. She wrote letters up and down her fingers or

palms with chokeberry ink, used the sweaty sides of a plow
horse for a blackboard and hunks of clay for chalk. Walnut
leaves helped her erase so she could start over if she made

a mistake. Bored, Todd squirms then tilts his head; I flash
cards. Perspective shifts: Z is N and N is Z. He asks if Z
with lines straight across is better than N with its height

and depth. He's safe if his back is horizontal and his feet
are vertical. Falls hurt less on the ground, but he won't stay
there forever, and so we experiment. Monkey up our tree,

I say. Swing out on a branch to throw down apples we can
eat, to let the juice run down our chins. Coring seeds to slice
half-moons, I resist a lecture on similes. We could dry fruit

for winter pies like my mother. Slivers browned into leather
on the silvery roof of the shed that kept in the smell of corn
my father stored there to treat the horses when it was cold.

Take a chance, I tell Todd. Climb up and we'll play catch,
challenge each other to a duel of peeling, find out who can
make the longest tissue thin curls. As we compete, I

might tell him how the tin roof drummed out marches
when it rained, slow steady like a funeral dirge and
how the snow came to cover it in a quiet as peaceful as

death is for one who believes. Asking what heaven looks
like, my son spreads out into the light as if he is trying to
ascend into air. I can picture Giotto's *Lamentation of Christ*,

where a flock of angels float in blue sky. Wings keep
them in flight but arms are yearning to touch earth,
to cradle the body below them in their hands just as

the mother does, her son in her lap, fingers cupping
his shoulders. Another woman is holding his wrist,
another lifts his feet as if to inspect the puncture

wounds. I could quote Dante's words about Giotto
from the *Purgatorio,* but we have to reach the last letter
of the alphabet before I can come up with an answer

for the question my son has asked. I tell him, picture all
the water in the world and then the smile on Noah's face
when he sees the zebras. That's how heaven will be.

A Glossary of Literary Terms for the Poet's Son

Two warring needs—the need to be accepted
and the need to be revenged
　　　—David Mamet

Sunday, leaving Grand Central Station, at 125th Street,
you stop, see your father running the New York City
Marathon. Keying train windows, waving a handkerchief
by a door, shouting his name, do not interrupt his pace.

Metaphor:　　　The train, window, marathon melt to
　　　　　　　a statue of the father you cannot touch

Simile:　　　　as if he were a limousine driver raising
　　　　　　　darkened glass after he drove off nineteen
　　　　　　　years ago. Seven, you did not understand.

Motif:　　　　Twenty-six, you understand. The phone
　　　　　　　call your father says he'll make next week,
　　　　　　　your dream each night. Dawn: promises

Pathos:　　　broken. I pile rhyme upon rhyme about
　　　　　　　love, time your father withheld that keeps
　　　　　　　you framed on his office desk as a child

Flashback:　　eyeing trophies awarded for the Boy Scout's
　　　　　　　Pine Car Derby at the VFW hall. Sanding,
　　　　　　　shellacking yellow flame decals down each
　　　　　　　side of your red car didn't keep wheels on.
　　　　　　　In the middle of the first heat, you cried,
　　　　　　　blamed me, the only mother there, for not
　　　　　　　being a father who'd know to secure axles.

Allegory:　　A Luna moth is trapped between the patio
　　　　　　　sliders. Pistachio wings pollen the glass like
　　　　　　　your hands on Amtrak's window. Thinking
　　　　　　　lepidoptery, a direction for your life, I point
　　　　　　　out the Luna's antennae are feathery like
　　　　　　　fronds of a fern, not clubbed like a butterfly.

Image:	A circle jewels each wing; I call four jade spots, outlined in black and yellow, eyes of God. Like your father on earth, a word, even one like heaven, can never be grasped, can never be embraced, unless it is physical.
Symbol:	Trying to escape, the Luna has torn one underwing just where it narrows to a tail. Like you, this moth is not a specimen for a display case. No athlete, totaling one Volvo then another, you were not perfect, shining like the trophy from a marathon.
Cliché:	Molasses fails to lure the moth from the doors. I light a candle, blow out the flame right before the Luna can singe its wings.

Programmed like a fibrillation, the relay medals matted
with 1964's picture of your father standing right next to
the Olympic torch in Tokyo, Japan, are a magnet for your
heart. Your fist through a door is literal, not figurative. Used
over and over like a cliché, your knuckles are raw, have
not lost adolescence. Fresh each day, rising like the sun,
your pain is as blinding as white light off chrome bumpers.

LETTER TO THE EDITOR WHO LABELED
THE POET *NAVEL GAZER*

Dear S.B. Startling me like your reply, Queen Anne's lace reflecting off my high beams trips my automatic dimmer, turns off my headlights. No Hatfield or McCoy, I don't hold a grudge, so I'll warn you not to go digging up parsley like foliage of this European weed just to suck the anemic carrot root. One close relative looks almost identical, though its stem is not hairy. Called poison hemlock, it killed Socrates. To show you I do own the *Oxford English Dictionary*, I will utilize the Latin derivative, *umbella*, for umbel rather than compare snowy clusters bunched on stalks of nearly equal length to ribs of an umbrella.

Without a large rolodex of names, or a vocabulary to gather each umbel that is pieced in hundreds of flowers, each with five petals, all I can see precisely is what is near to me. To demonstrate that research does go into navel gazing, let me explain that the psychological term for this is *closure*, which means the mind finishes the image, filling in details, without having to actually examine them. Illustrating my ability to magnify specifics, I will start by observing that the outermost layer of petals on Queen Anne's lace is stitched a full three-eighths of an inch longer than the middle rows. To satisfy your need for documentation, I'll even include the two female parts in the heart that stiffen to keep company with one floret of purple-red because I can footnote the legend. Every time Britain's Queen Anne, patron of lace makers, picked up a needle, she pricked her finger and the center is her blood.

If I were a meteorologist, I might observe that in dry weather outer stems bend out, then if moist, they lean in so pollinated seeds can spiral in the wind. In case you might be impressed by my knowledge of math, let me add the geometry of fractals. One mile of the meandering Cumberland River is the template for its entire pattern, just as the jaggedness of mountain ridges near my home equals that of the Appalachian range. In fact, I do not have to handle each and every redwood to see Sequoia, or each umbel of Queen Anne's lace to see a weed patch in bloom. Respectfully, Vivian.

Foxfire: Why the Poet Holds onto the Past

Ten years now, I've come to Howe Valley, the church
graveyard, but my father's stubbled face will not recede
beneath plane wings like white fences of Calumet Farms

framing Kentucky's Blue Grass Airport do. It's the hour
for witches to take up broomsticks, but I have no coven,
augury or incantation to dam this sudden rogue wave

of grief. I know nomenclature of root salves but three
fingers of bourbon will ease my flight to Connecticut.
To keep him in my life, I've worn my father's Pendleton

cardigan threadbare but it's not unraveling. Digging in
his heels when he went to stop a horse and plow, he
did not believe in quiet passage, no kicking, clawing

or hollering, but his heart did take its own sweet time
to stop. Slaughtering pigs, chickens, knowing death
first hand, my father was angry about what he was

losing: creek stone walls he had built, bacon grease
wilting dandelion greens, lathes, drills, oak, black walnut
boards in his cellar that would go to hands that never

climbed them as trees in Hardin County. My father
showed me how a mountain lion tracks a dotted line as
if on a tightrope, that coyotes stagger dog prints, pointed

out a hen turkey topping a tree to shake apples down
to her flock. Why is it that what I'm thinking about is
poking rotten poplar stumps on the farm to unearth

an inverted castle lit by foxfire? I doubt my father was
teaching me about conservation of energy absorbed by
luminous fungus molecules that must reappear again

in some form. More likely, it was a lesson about love
for those no longer on this earth, how grief must find
a voice. Buried it will decay like foxfire, will not glow

until it's broken up and gets air. My father knew its history:
in Scotland and Ireland foxfire was called fairy fire,
will-o-the wisp, Jack-with-a-lantern. Cherokees named it

cold fire because it's bluish-green, wet, burning, oxidizing
to emit light. Jewels by night, luciferase, an enzyme,
caused decaying wood to glow. Never in walnut, pine or fir,

by day it was watermarked by circles and black lines called
spalling. I had read how Tom Sawyer and Huck Finn
planned to dig an escape tunnel to the cabin where

the slave Jim was being held. A lantern would have
given them away; they looked for *them rotten chunks that's
called foxfire and just makes a soft kind of glow when you lay them*

in a dark place. Not trying to free anyone, just wanting
some fun, my father and I would get buckets of foxfire
to throw into Rough Creek. Like sorrow that tears won't

wash away, water will not quench it. Over waterfalls,
down currents, chunks broke up and went for half a mile
until the whole creek was lit up like it was Christmas.

It has taken me most of a lifetime to have a heart that
can subtract from itself and still beat. Writing poems
about my father, his untrimmed brows like lichen-moss,

is like stringing bits and pieces of foxfire on leaves and
branches so they can dip and move to light a way for me
as they did for Huck and Jim through the woods, the night.

A LETTER UNSETTLES THE POET

With my yo-yo, I walk the dog and go clear around
the world, but otherwise, I stand still, look at weed

and bramble. Slitting the envelope, I read that my friend
is taking off for Europe Tuesday, a look at Wimbledon,

a Scandinavian cruise before she begins to study
at Oxford. Her daughters will travel with boyfriends

from Paris to Rome and then explore Italy on their own.
She'll join them for a long weekend in Geneva, then

back to England for a theater course. Imagine, six hours
of credit for going to plays in London with Roger Reese,

Derek Jacobi and Ben Kingsley! Oh yes, her lecture
at the Folger in Washington went well. It was elegant—

an occasion—one of many she has been allowed to enjoy.
I haven't been anywhere yet, but it's on my list: *let's get*

*this act on the road; girl, shake a leg; let's get cracking; I am
clearing out of here.* If I go too fast, I won't see anything.

If I slow down, I won't be here to see everything before
it disappears as the horizon does, a line like black spots

by the sides of my eyes. Turn full faced, they're gone.
At a mosque in Damietta, there is a column of pumice.

If I lick it until my tongue bleeds, it must bleed, I will be
cured of restlessness. Such choices: spots like my friend's

letter that suck at my eyes or tongues that must bleed. It is
easier to stay put, leave the mail unopened, than to plead:

take me along like floss for your teeth or bifocals you
never wear. I'll be light, no more weight than a paper sack.

Fading like pink liliums, no ardor carries me through July;
everything holds its position: a manuscript, a chair, computer

but no printer. Perhaps if I could afford to travel, stay on
in Dover when hotels are shutting, umbrellas are folded,

I'd decide I didn't want to join my friend in London or Paris,
but read Maxine Kumin in a library by *Maison Dieu*, stand

by chalk cliffs that trace the coast. Listening for a gull's call,
waiting to watch light shining on the Strait, there would be

eighteen miles of English Channel for me to cross, opening
like years or the gulf between France, my friend and me.

A Winning Number, the Poet Replies

You haven't been to Prague, yet?

Gerald Stern, Adam Michnik
Grace Paley, Edward Hirsch
Alan Levy, Vance Bourjaily
Ivan Klima, William Gass

Shall we go on?

Held at historic Charles University
in July, this workshop is the answer
to your writer's block. Just imagine
lying on your back on a long stretch
of green, a cup of Merlot—or Perrier,
if you prefer—cooling at your side.
Watch a white owl circle and dive
from deep blue to lift a gray mouse,
a piece of wheat still clutched in teeth.
This could be the natural event, color,
you have searched for. Roll over, pick
up your Montblanc, position your pad
of parchment on your knees, allow
the heat of your body to rise, to ignite
your words. Calligraph another poem.

Give us a call to find out more:
1-800-INSPIRE.

What are you waiting for?

WHY THE AGING POET SIGNS UP
FOR A SUMMER POETRY WORKSHOP

I'm inspired by Red Pollard who was also told
he lacked the talent to justify the torture. Red should
have been a poet, not a jockey poring over Emerson
and Omar Khayyam. Too tall, he starved himself

until he fainted, put on a rubber suit and buried
himself in fermenting manure piles to sweat off
pounds, swallowed eggs of tapeworms that hatched
to eat the food he squirreled away. Less squeamish

or light enough to race, I would have been called
hardboot, a name given to Kentuckians on tracks
all over the country. Like an old shoe molded
to only one foot, I do have a thick hide that's held up

through years of nettling by tongues of other poets.
Unlike my rondeaus and pantoums, Red somersaulted
into history on August 16, 1936, a jockey, down
to twenty-seven cents and a flask of *bow-wow wine.*

Red gave a sugar cube to Seabiscuit, a battered
racehorse, a kindred soul like one I hope to find
on the conference faculty at Wesleyan. Like ham
curing on a hook, my heart still swings from

Connecticut to Kentucky. Writing poems about barns
holding wood shavings from my father's knife,
stains of tobacco he spit on the floor will be like
spitting cherry stones out to breadcrumb my way

home to hills of Howe Valley. In workshops, I will
maintain Red's dignity and smile, not be defeated
by being labeled *easy to read,* and *plain of speech,*
or *ordinary.* Unlike Red, I was never abandoned

at fifteen on a racetrack cut into a Montana hayfield.
There has never been any need for me to thumb
through *Job* to cheer up. Because my feet grounded
in bluegrass generations ago, I'd had my chances,

but never rode bad horses by day or slept in their stalls
by night after getting punched bloody by cow-town
boxers. So, Red would be my subject for the list poem
on the summer syllabus: chest crushed, left eye blinded,

leg almost sheared off, teeth kicked out, back and skull
fractured. Until Seabiscuit's last race—March 2, 1940
at Santa Anita—Red had said they *were a couple of old
cripples together, all washed up* but they rode to victory,

drawing a crowd of 78,000. I can picture myself reading
this poem to them. A hardboot like Red, I refuse to believe
my hopes exceed what nature and fate bestowed. There is
always revision, maybe even a change in literary taste.

WEEK FOUR: THE POET WRITES ABOUT ANOTHER PERSON

Winter hardens New Haven. Wind that chips at sleeves
and pockets makes men like Tony who croon syllables to
muscatel then piss behind stairways on Howe Street, sad

to have hands. There were years when Tony had enough
to rent a room at the Taft Hotel. Spring days, he would lean
out of a window in a sleeveless undershirt. Now, he's lucky

if he gets to sleep at Viva Zapata on rice bags the cooks store
in piles near a furnace to keep them dry. Most days, Tony
has his own stool at the bar in Rudy's on the corner of Elm

and Howe. The bartender, Marty, lets him use the john
with enough light to read handwriting of a twenty year old
Yalie who doesn't care enough to dot the *i* or cross the *t*.

I'm a regular and from a state school across town. It's okay
if I buy Tony's story for my poem by picking up his tab
for Jack Daniels and Sam Adams he normally can't afford.

Tactful, I make mental notes as I ask, *What makes you drink
so hard, do a shot, a beer, a shot, a beer at nine in the morning?* Tony
mumbles about Champion Auto, how he operated two bays,

two at one time. Listening, a girl with a bulldog on her hat,
drinks coffee, leans back on a wall plastered with Whaler's
banners, Raven's baseballs, football photos from Yale Bowl.

To show her what I know, how clever I can be, I quote
Drink? or think? better drink. Charles Bukowski is dead
and there's a spot I can fill. No need for me to live the lines.

For the price of another round, I gather authentic detail,
get Tony to talk about how he tried to end World War II
by cutting his wrists, but bleeding was too slow. Each shot

of whiskey brings him closer to the bar, face fallen forward.
Some days he cuts his forehead, but the bouncer lets him sit,
drink beer as long as he's good for the business at Rudy's.

The owners, Michael and Hank, have left orders about what
to do if Tony shakes his fist and starts to mutter, *You
goddamn Yalie! I operated two bays at one time, two bays at one time.*

Friday Tea: the Poet
Opens the Manuscript Vault
at Yale's Elizabethan Club

Afraid I will sneeze, I won't touch a First Folio
of Shakespeare offered by Beinecke Library's curator.
Should I explore—as an academic question, of course—

the purity in Elizabethan speech of people confined
to Appalachian cricks and hollers? Leaving Kentucky
for New Haven, I knew my syllables would unwind,

spill to entangle and mark me like a blue ribbon stuck
on the prize pig at a state fair. Trying to forget the lope
of my accent like a pink shawl crocheted by my Aunt Hazel

I had deliberately left on a chair, I shortened vowels, pulling
at imaginary strings with my tongue, extended diphthongs
with a tuck of my jawbone. Still, like signals from men

trapped in Harlan County mines, there were words clawing
in me. In the club library, I watch a man drink Earl Grey tea,
his little finger a comma, and I think of my Uncle Paul,

with a soft rag of voice but no nobleman's British accent,
who was so polite he held a cup to his lips to catch
tobacco juice instead of spitting. I want to hear the hillbilly

in my voice, reclaim parcels of my life that I had needed
to keep tied. A real *gosh darn it*, this afternoon I might say
a-sittin' and *a-rockin'* without explaining that the use

of the *a* prefix strictly before verbs ending in *ing* turns
out to be consistent in mountain dialect. As I describe
that *ole woman stumblin' up that there hill with a poke*

and a pig walkin' right beside her, my father saying, *let me*
ride behind you on that, meaning save me the sure bet,
all the members surely will circle me in the garden to hear

a fur piece
no ready mades
a handed-down story
young'uns
tomorry at sunrise.

If I don't lose my audience while reading my new poem
about our outhouse, using an old Sears Roebuck catalogue
for toilet paper, maybe just one member of the Lizzy will cry

Forever more!

Vocabulary Lesson for the Poet

I go stumbling (head turned) back to my origins
— Denise Levertov

Humiliated, I take aim with the camera and click to show
my father how he looks in four shirts and pants hitched
up, standing out in the rain feeding sparrows as if they were
chickens he taught me how to hypnotize. My mother called
him *a caution, a ring-tailed caution.* The baby sitter next door
wouldn't let him in, called to warn me about a character
wandering around. Tact, concern for his safety don't work;
he says he gets about just fine in the dark, has owl's blood;
some dogs just keep their noses to ground and see nothing
over their heads. Not him. Kiss me, he'd say. Taste wildness
of survivors: ginseng, paw paws, arrow wood, root of ginger.

We toss horseshoes on Saturdays. He can't see the stake but
his arm remembers how to pitch ringers. A country man
in bib overalls wiped with cow manure, his hands jutted out
rubbing denim. My father could sit without thinking, moving
only to wipe his mouth after spitting. Endless days, powdered
dirt clouded my bare feet running for Nellie, a plow horse
who knew to puff her stomach, keep a saddle loose when she
inhaled. Kick her so the strap will stay, my father shouted,
bend to cinch the girth, dodge teeth aiming for a shoulder.
January mornings, I watched him warm the bit in his palm
to keep it from sticking to Snip's mouth, mutilate his tongue.
Tail hair was used to restring a fiddle so we could play along
with the Opry, Hank Snow saying: *Good night. Good luck.*
Good health. May the good Lord always be proud of you. To teach
me a lesson, Hank should have substituted *daughter* for *Lord.*
I didn't need a dictionary to learn my father's vocabulary:

    i.   *seasons:* setting was done by Decoration Day, cutting
                Labor Day weekend and stripping by Thanksgiving.

    ii.   *discipline:* tight bales.

iii.	*foresight:* a few hands of tobacco, dry and stripped from stems, crumbled into a nail keg to flesh out Brown Mule chewing tobacco, Duke's Mixture.
iv.	*awaken:* how to tease the appetite in steel by using a whetstone to sharpen a blade for cutting hay.
v.	*luxury:* cutting out just the hearts of Rocky Ford watermelons lying out in the field and eating them in the moonlight.
vi.	*pride:* frying eggs for white bread when men would come knocking at the back door, looking for work.
vii.	*cruelty:* torching spiders.
viii.	*contentment:* old rams butting heads like aging lovers.
ix.	*survival:* holding a rifle light as cottonwood. Coming up real slow, not aiming too long, shooting fast.
x.	*evasion:* jumping pools of tobacco juice spit by men lining Elizabethtown's courthouse.

These ten words stay with me, fossiled like limestone
my father stacked into fences until his arthritic hands gave
in and he stapled wire to trees. Bark has grown over barbs.
Filled with silt of years, the pond is too shallow to surface
for breath. My father used to make me sit on the edge,
let bluegills take a bobber and run before I set the hook, but
the last time we fished, he kept reeling in, moving his bait
as if impatient for the strike to come. Leading him by an arm
from my backyard, I let him talk on about getting up before
sunrise to clean a plow he pushed breaking ruts in fields.
My father knew about the appetite of dirt for corn he flung
as if he were a poet scattering words, trying to seed the earth.

THE POET IN A BLACK HOLE

Was your mind vacant like Harlan County mine shafts or
dark as Mammoth Cave's lake when the tour guide flicked
off light? I grabbed for you, Uncle Justus; you leaned back
in the boat's seat. Your silence taunts me like the quarrel you
wouldn't join in when I blurted out I couldn't help it you
and my father only had girls, that I wasn't the boy you both

wanted. Knowing you had no use for poetry, to show science
I'd learned, I rattled on about black holes, dense clumps
of mass in outer space with gravitational force so strong stars,
meteors, gas clouds and even light were sucked in, as I was
by hope of just a nod from you. You were fingering the top
you'd whittled, but I continued right on hoping to startle you

with a list of statistics, how the holes might contain over
two billion suns, that Albert Einstein predicted them in 1915,
even though he had no way of proving the identity of one
until the Hubble Space Telescope could spot whirlpools
of stars as they were snuffed out. Certain as the scientists
of density I couldn't see, sure there must be a black hole

behind creases above your eyes, I tried to settle my hook
with talk of *Star Trek*, how time and space could stretch,
twist, tear or loop for trips in other eras and dimensions.
Not even waiting to hear my grand finale, how the only way
to escape a black hole was to travel faster than the speed
of light, you called out to my father, in from the back field,

that, finally, you had figured out how to pick out Queenie's
hunting mouth from her treed mouth. When you slumped
gray faced over the tractor, you made no sound, left no word
for me resting on your tongue like communion cubes before
the preacher gives the congregation a signal to swallow
the bread, transformed into flesh by the need for human love.

III

Is the Poet *Walling In* or *Walling Out?*

We have to use a spell to make them balance
— Robert Frost

Unexpected, this Connecticut day melting
winter, seasons still locked in the ground.
False Spring, my neighbor calls out to me
as I watch him rebuild our boundary wall,
bind the land with thriftiness of line. The top
is already spilling over into the dirt; flat rocks
bend down as if yearning to avalanche.

Rehearsed in lifting gravity, realizing that
earth does not repent, then cast out stones,
he points out boulders that his numbed hands
will pry. We can see there is no final resting,
that our spring ritual is just like putting out
a leaking pan to catch rain water for my hair.

Knowing I will never be a Robert Frost,
my neighbor is my friend because he takes
me and my poetry seriously. It's my job
to watch, to comment, maybe write heroic
couplets about his skill. Never one to shirk duty,
aware of what I will provoke in him, I offer,
Odd, the history in unhewn, unmarked stone.

Sure enough, he stops wedging pieces of granite
that are worn to pink, not speckled in gray
like the photograph his uncle took of his father
standing by the base of the Statue of Liberty.
My neighbor never tires of pulling the picture
from his wallet and talking about the statue,
how its foundation is built of our same pink
Stony Creek granite. His grandfather quarried it
in Branford, blasting sections to cut for engineers
with their charts that were fortification against

frost that heaves the earth. Tired out from all
of his work, I decide to leave my neighbor here.

In the morning, I'll ask him how he would describe
our wall when muffled in snow or fringed in grass.
Sunset is the good hour for him, spent watching
red tailed hawks float, never measuring days
in hours taken to tie stalks of corn as my father did.
I used to watch Daddy gaze skyward, appearing
to measure Howe Valley fields out of his reach.
I wonder if, after all, my father was a poet looking
for stones, for a light to guide him through.

The Poet, Snowed In

This weather could make me manic.
Light, thin as an invalid's broth,
is rationed out to be sipped as if there
were no hunger for forsythia gnawing me.
No willow with iced dreadlocks, I'm
like an old fir that will snap after bending
too long. Awake, I suspect there must be
an ode or elegy buried out there. White birch
with Shelley's promise budding their limbs
If winter comes, can spring be far behind?
are not enough to see me through February.
I can quote poetry, but I don't have a degree
from Yale. With a diploma in my hand
I could have joined Mory's, been an old blue
like my Christmas spruce. Evergreen,
I might have seen this storm coming
and hunkered down, all backbone. Instead,
I need a jug of Kentucky moonshine,
white lightning to jolt my bones, to jazz
the arborvitae that have stayed stooped
for months. Their curved backs spell April
pruning, or even uprooting if I'm not sober.

Sleeping Soundly with the Poet
Where Lizzie Borden Did

From fields where glory does not stay
— A. E. Housman

Ambiguity, an unsolved murder case from a hot August day in 1892, have lured me. That and the chance to sleep in the bed of a thirty-two year old woman, and a Sunday school teacher to boot, who might have taken an axe and killed her seventy year old father with ten blows to the head and her stepmother with nineteen. Lizzie is the only Fall River, Massachusetts woman modern and famous enough to have her very own homepage on the World Wide Web: www.Lizzie-Borden.com. She's even a part of the *Welcome to the City* page: *What do Lizzie Borden and Molten Metal Technology have in common? Both used cutting-edge technology.*

At the Lizzie Borden Bed and Breakfast Museum, I can sleep in Lizzie's room, or the one in which Abby, her stepmother, was murdered. For the faint hearted, there's The Bridget Sullivan Room, named for the Borden's maid who discovered the bodies. Those who want to be protected by the law can nap with pictures of the family attorney in the Andrew Jennings Room, or the district attorney in Hosea Knowlton's Room. Lights flicker, video equipment turns on then off, cameras work when they shouldn't and don't work when they should. All this and the Borden's last meal of eggs, sausages, home fries, johnny cakes, cornbread and bananas with mutton broth for $219 a night. Plus, there are sugar cookies shaped like axes for the ride home.

This Greek Revival house is no Cinderella fabrication from Disney, it's the actual site of two murders. This New England industrial town of brick fortresses with boards for windows is no set from Universal. Stench of Troy Cotton and Woolen Manufactory is gone. Stafford Mills is drained of men and women so tired they groaned getting into bed like a hull bruising against barnacles. Stacks of letters bundled with rubber bands are all that's left of Durfee Mills. I find the pages, brittle as insect wings, when I go to the Historical Society to do research for my poem. More exciting is the yellowed trial tag reading Mr. Borden's stomach. Yes, I'm disappointed red gobs on the tag turn out to be sealing wax, but spots on Abby Borden's bedspread and her pillowcase are real enough, like the skulls, or what's left of them.

What I admire most about Lizzie is her creativity, willingness to revise. Following like fish in a school, her stories all started with she hadn't heard a thing. When the murders occurred: she had been out in the barn eating pears when her stepmother went up to the guest room to change the linens; she was out in the barn looking for fishing sinkers; she was in the dining room ironing and folding handkerchiefs while her father was murdered, as he catnapped in the sitting room ten feet away. Only a few stains were on her dress, but she burned it the following day in the kitchen stove. Maybe she wasn't getting rid of evidence, but had a poet's sensitive soul and couldn't bear to wear her father's blood and was just too tired to do washing.

Arrested, no prayer or rosary circling her wrist. There was no way she would confess—like granite, conceded nothing. The judge was no pulley and winch, coaxing Lizzie, convincing her inch by inch with talk of ropes. After a thirteen day trial, she was acquitted in one hour. Maybe the jury wanted to believe her story, couldn't imagine a woman, the daughter of a prosperous furniture merchant, no less, would commit such a crime. It sure is a real pity that even one juror had not visited Cecelia, Kentucky, to watch my cousin give our hog a sharp blow on the head with an axe while her sister stuck him in the jugular, about three inches back from the left jawbone. Understanding the power hidden in a woman's arm, the accuracy of her aim, the jury might have realized Lizzie possessed the will, the strength, to raise an axe twenty-nine times.

A boat built with dry wood takes up water and never gives it up; Lizzie showed no sign of grief to melt neighboring hearts. Shunned for life, never weighted by remorse, Lizzie was like a dory built with green wood so water wouldn't seep in. Fit enough to row alone out into the ocean, she endured until 1927, and was buried in her family plot. Unlike other women whose days are condensed on a gravestone, and chiseled with a man's last name, Lizzie Borden's name stays alive on tongues of poets that come seeking authentic detail by licking plates she might have used.

Cleaning, cooking and canning died with the good deeds of Fall River wives and nothing of life preserved the hard way is displayed in the Historical Society, not even hair locketed in gold. No bottled bathwater labeled *Lizzie* is sold for those who made chicken and dumplings materialize in their hands. Poets like me come to Oak Grove Cemetery to lean on an axe handle, not to count how many years were spent weeding gardens with no hope of bloom. Not one hand reaches to finger the names resting on pain of childbirth, lasting like a laurel, like a rose.

Unable to Revise the Canon, the Poet Finds George Sterling

Stand on a street corner in the Tenderloin. The search
begins with an embrace. A swift ballet, your wallet
is gone. The round trip ticket from San Francisco is still

in your hotel room with a flight number, departure date
and time. This is a break. Call American Express but don't
move to a different hotel. You can get a free tweed jacket

at the Salvation Army in the Outer Mission. Throw it over
your left shoulder like George Sterling did, and on
Sixteenth Street you can go underground, become invisible

for a few hours or for a few days. How lucky you had
your wallet lifted. Otherwise, to achieve this sensation,
you'd have to give twenties, fifties and finally hundreds

to more and more men who warm the street before you can
go deeper into the Mission to bargain for a carne asada
burrito at the Roosevelt Tamale Parlor, or buy a hex cooped

up in either ointment, a candle or aerosol. At first, you
should do nothing more daring than go to the Castro and sip
an espresso at the Cafe Flore. Build up to working the spell

you bought into a triple: slide into North Beach and steal
back the twentieth century, evaporate from a Barbary Coast
saloon, solidify in an opium den. You'll find George Sterling

seated, sharing a water pipe with Robinson Jeffers. Be sure
to save enough magic to get back home so you can hike up
Telegraph Hill, walking on wooden boards to the shanties

that brought Kerouac such joy. Push even shove through
commuters waiting for the bus by a red striped curb right
under the big gold letters of City Lights Bookstore. Its

doors shoulder plate glass that protects pyramids of *Howl*
and *On the Road*. Edge down to the basement, plug a tape
in you smuggled all the way back from the Barbary Coast:

George Sterling reciting *Lilith* and *Testimony of the Suns*.
Inhale absinthe, or drink the Medoc stuffed behind the dark
narrow shelves and let the fog outside digest you. Then go

deeper, deeper where the census taker never polls. Ducks
ribbon King Tin Restaurant; resist them. Avert your head
from the ichthyosaurs on crushed ice. To seek Sterling, you

must go further, even further to the last room fragrant with
perilla, rape seed, sesame and mustard. Open the thirteenth
drawer of the acupuncturist Sterling consulted for old pain;

see what is desiccated. When he was here, the signage was
all different, the streets, the restaurant aisles much too close.
There was no one to wire money from home. Don't give up

yet. No tourist now, you know to bend your knees to live
through an earthquake. To find Sterling, tuck yourself into
the top of Russian Hill. Pose as a flower poking through

the laurel leaves that filter cruise ships going from the bay
into the Pacific. When it is exactly one half hour before
sunset, while there is still time to see, go to the end of

a path. You will know the one; it is overgrown. What you
will find is rather small, a stone cut in the only words by
George Sterling left in San Francisco that you can touch:

*Tho' the dark be cold and blind, Yet the sea fog's touch
is kind, And her mightier caress Is Joy and the pain
thereof; And great is thy tenderness, cool gray city of love.*

THE POET PICTURES
EMILY DICKINSON AS QUILTER

Unhooked from words, Emily turned to quilting. Organizing days by color rather than outline, purple provided a thread, sometimes in synonyms of iodine, amethyst and tyrian. Emily had strict rules: never stitch a quilt on Friday; never make one lacking a flaw; put in a missing block, a stuttered braid or attach an extra row. Since only God was perfect, Emily deliberately misplaced shapes or patches of color to display her faith. Stacks of quilts, tied into packets like poems, were piled edge to center, floor to ceiling in her bedroom. To clear air of death, Emily's sister, Lavinia, flooded first Amherst then other parts of Massachusetts with patterns her older sister crafted. Doing what she could to create order in her life, Emily numbered quilts as if they were a sequence of poems.

141

Evening Star was piled on the top. Used to wrap the dead, if it was a last wish, Emily did not express it to Lavinia. Backed in cast off linen, pieces of her mother's wedding gown were framed in black velvet from the dress Emily had worn to mourn father, mother and her brother Austin's child. Scrapping fifty years of Dickinson life, Emily stitched from heart to mind *Tenderly tucking them in from frost / Before their feet are cold.*

214

No member of the Women's Christian Temperance Union, *the Debauchee of Dew* stitched a spiky track shaded in black called Drunkard's Path, not for husbands she watched as they staggered home, but to celebrate self and drinking rum: Domingo, Jamaica, *the little Tippler / From Manzanilla come!*

249

Wrapped in Mariner's Compass, with a complex star of many diamonds she worked around pineapples, Emily shipped out with sailors bound for the South Seas: *Futile- the Winds- / To a Heart in port- / Done with the Compass- / Done with the Chart!*

398

At first glance, Lavinia might have seen stars in her older sister's Spiderweb quilt. Emily varied pieces in webs to get different effects. *A limit like the Veil / Unto the lady's face- / But every Mesh-a Citadel- / And Dragons-in the Crease-.*

945

Blossom of the Brain- / A small -italic Seed / Lodged by Design or Happening was stitched in Grandmother's Flower Garden, hexagons of blue, yellow, pink and green Emily leaned over on the fence to watch her sister-in-law, Sue, tend every spring.

956

To have something to help her face tomorrow's question, *I-do not fly, so wherefore / My Perennial Things?* Emily left the tricky Feather Star and Indian Braids in sequence, unfinished.

986

The evil Emily knew, she met more than once on walks and quilted it into the Snake: *But never met this Fellow / Attended, or alone / Without a tighter breathing / And Zero at the Bone-.*

1142

Creating her own home, she stitched Log Cabin with red wool at the center of each square for a fire to consume strips of a dress she cut up for logs. Crooked and pitched, the pieces were rectangles used as props until *The House support itself / And cease to recollect / The Augur and the Carpenter-.*

1247

To calculate a change in season, *To pile like Thunder to its close / Then crumble grand away,* Emily set green and white triangles into eight squares combined with a green and white square to make four corner blocks. Quilted, white triangles formed Weathervane made of 21 blocks alternating with 21 planes.

1483

As covert as a Fugitive, / Cajoling Consternation / By Ditties to the Enemy / And Sylvan Punctuation- not in her words, but in the deeds she stitched, Emily was no stranger to the Civil War. She hung Jacob's Ladder on her mother's clothesline to give the runaway slaves who could not read a code that the Dickinson house was a safe one.

1732

Not to cover any woman, her Friendship Quilt was for Charles Wadsworth when he left for San Francisco. To let her fingers show her love, her skill, Emily embroidered in all the stitches she knew: herringbone, arrowhead, feathered chain, chevron. She didn't thread a tract of names Charles was leaving behind, but *Parting is all we know of heaven, / And all we need of hell.*

Quilting small pieces of Amherst life, love or renunciation, ecstasy or suffering, doing what she could to stop age, make the time pass, Emily would not have displayed her quilts. Exposure to sunlight, while it enriched life, faded the color, weakened fabric. What Lavinia did find in her sister's room were poems, 1,775 packets of them folded in chests, perched on chairs, stacked at the foot of Emily's bed. Because Lavinia did not burn her sister's poems, they were canonized like relics from a saint. With patchwork tented over knees or stretched on a frame, if Emily had stitched *This is my letter to the world / That never wrote to Me-* on quilted cloth, and never inked a poem, her life would have been folded into chests, numberless like days of other women and be left nameless, to rot.

LOOKING AT JAMES MERRILL'S POEMS
UNMOORS THE POET

He is dead and it is a mistake to read *The Victor Dog* out
loud to my class. My voice tears but not over, *Obediently,*
in silence like the grave's / He sleeps there. I falter because

of the life I have postponed, what I will never have. Winter
after winter, I put off going to readings, seeing that smile
like a bird's wing give his words flight. I heard Merrill's voice

only once, floating like an aria from Celeste Bartos Forum's
ceiling as the conclusion to Merrill's May memorial service
at the New York Public Library. Squeezed into a row behind

his mother, Stanley Kunitz to my left, I was with an invited
guest, not masquerading as a mourner. Pasting faces onto
poets' names, I listened to stories about Jimmy, shifting in

my seat while Kyoko Saito sang Berlioz and Faure. I can't
regather life I have missed: sitting beside Merrill at Yale,
in rooms at Silliman or seeing him at the Metropolitan Opera

in mauve Birkenstocks and lime green socks with Navajo
turquoise buckling his waist. Spring or fall, he wore pressed
corduroys, Venetian bow tie, Gap shirt; in winter, a loden

cape, baseball cap. Visiting his ashes last August was not
the same. No need for a granite marker with verses carved
from *Luke* or a cannon to fire into dark, his grave is not a sad

one, not one for a child. Space Merrill takes in earth is small,
a miniature of his life like a blue marble painted with green
continents that was dropped into his grave. An outcropping

of rock is at his feet and there is no way to know how people
surrounding him were released into this earth: the Webbs,
Stuart Weston and Marcia Sewall with their daughter Elinor,

1927-32. Barbara Johnstone is beside George A., the second
husband of Marcia W. Did they fight the entry, bitter, angry,
not ready to let go of Stonington lobster, waves, stone walls

marking space? *The last chord fades* as if James Merrill was
a metronome that stopped music. Merrill was past middle
years. I don't know if he outlived yearning that dreams carry,

when desire is worth the burning in the dark. The pulse of his
heart was strong, a heavyweight punching, solid, like years
that passed me one after the other. If I had listened, rhythm

must have varied. His beat stopped. There was not another.
If only he'd rise from flames to riffle paper I pass out, but
he can't conjugate verbs in language that has no future tense.

WHY THE POET VISITS
JAMES MERRILL'S GRAVE

In Connecticut, when the Latin King Arsomo Diaz
from Fair Haven was gunned down, his street name

Ra-Ra was spray painted in red to cover the spot.
No chiseled letters mark your ashes, just a wooden

cross, handmade from two sticks streaked in green
and thonged by maroon leather. A sign reads:

Stonington Cemetery Incorporated 1849. Diamond
rectangles pattern two wrought iron gates that

have been left akimbo. At the Hyde granite obelisk,
I bear left; at Erskine M. Phelps' Greek temple,

I go right. Paths are not human ones rutted out
by feet, but by the years giving in to natural contours

of land. There's been no rain for twenty-five days
and only a four wheel could get through to you when

storms come. In spite of drought, brushfires consuming
Long Island, moss blanketing your grave is green,

sheltered as it is by two oaks. I have no need here
for clouds buoyed like prayer to give me intermittent

shelter from the sun. Hanging over the geranium and
dusty miller crowded in plastic clay bracing the cross,

three low branches of the closest live oak are barren.
I'm too heavy, too old to shimmy up the trunk and break

them off. I find a fence I can climb. Toting a pole saw,
I'll come back after the caretaker leaves at dusk, because

the sign at the front entry reads: *Any person desiring
to plant or remove other than flowers shall obtain the approval*

of the Superintendent. I know cold will numb the thickened
trunk, amputating dead limbs like spears of ice that could

unhinge to pierce your grave. My concern is not about
the surface, or that your spot will be forgotten, but that

shoveled from the flames, your body which left so much
in this world, should rest in sun that lights Sandover's end.

EXCERPTS BY THE POET
OF T. S. ELIOT'S BIRTHDAY
LETTERS TO EZRA POUND
IN ST. ELIZABETH'S HOSPITAL
FOR THE CRIMINALLY INSANE

I. Ezra Pound's 61st Birthday
                    October 30, 1946

You, Ezra, there in St. Elizabeth's are a burr
on the base of my brain. Remembering yourself
as old, the poet folding blankets in his tent, you recall
a soldier who built you a table out of packing cases
for ammunition, how you kept your promise, did not
tell the guard. I resolve to get you released, restore
order to your life, snatch what we can from years
that remain; you urge young racists to take the streets,
cheer for white supremacy, burn crosses. How can
I keep my vow, remove the labels of *anti-Semite*
and *racist* billboarding you? I'm concerned about
the actual, your teeth, your food, your room, television
going full blast, inmates sleeping in corridors, hollow
eyes acting out their own mad theater. A man next
door beats his wall, rhythm like Joe Louis punching
steady, steady, hard like mounting years will be.

II. Ezra Pound's 62nd birthday
                    October 30, 1947

Broadcasting as Uncle Ez, you windmilled your arms
like you do if I speak when I should not, but then
I don't think insanity should be your whole defense.
Labeled *radio traitor* with Tokyo Rose, your broadcasts
were in the style of your *Canto*s, guarantee you would
not be understood. Images jutting out like rocks in
a drying creek, you jumped from Hitler to Confucius,

from 1750, the Pennsylvania Colony's suppression
of paper money, to Cleopatra. *Querulous, egocentric,*
grandiose and distractible. He is in other words insane.
What psychiatrists meant as madness in 1945 was not
dementia, but your fury coupled with a mind skipping
over what it knew. Down St. Elizabeth's main hall,
just past security lights, hospital fans sigh, creating
undertow that sucks air to where it is unbreathable.
Cooled, it drops like memory, dreams of your father,
the U.S. Mint. Melting down gold, drawing crucibles,
skimming, pouring molten light, I bring you birthday
flame to slice blinds, yellowed wax on wood, worn to
skin by your left foot under the table where you write.

III. Ezra Pound's 63rd birthday
                              October 30, 1948

And how did it first happen, our attraction?
Both of us engulfed by World War I, the slaughter,
sure that the heartwood of our world was rotten, we
were seeking the solution, a new salvation. I was
fresh out of a Swiss psychiatric rest home, Tom Eliot,
clerk at Lloyds Bank. 1921. You slashed away
at the poem I carried, badgered me into carving out
whole stanzas, pages from *The Waste Land* trying
to push up like fescue. Ezra, it was as if you held
grass blades to your lips, whistled and one half
of my poem followed, sentences flying out, ribbons
on a pole. Copernicus muttered about Mars, why
it seemed to stray. Newton first saw what we know,
how friends are drawn together as if the sun were
pulling us in curves, elliptical, slow, at times
moving off in the sweeping motion of a wanderling.

IV. Ezra Pound's 64th birthday
                              October 30, 1949

Ezra, it is time for you to let go of memory, anger,
of fists rapping, being handcuffed in your courtyard
at Rapallo. 1943. Three weeks of Mediterranean

summer outside Pisa, guards folded you into a cage
measuring 6' by 6' made of metal matting used
for airfield runways. Forbidden to speak, parched
by bright light shone through bars at night, you did
not know where the morning, the afternoon crossed.
Finally given a sleeping tent, like a shadow boxer,
you fenced with a broomstick, helped illiterate
prisoners compose letters home, giving them
your solution for all humanity: *Mussolini.* Cleaning
muck out of life, your idol would control traffic
by curving streets, feed Italy by growing peanuts.
In *The Pisan Cant*os, you would not back away
from being the funnel for Mussolini who was like
a magnet through a mirror exerting force on iron
filings scattered on glass. No *rose in the steel dust,*
Mussolini was executed in Milan, his head
hanging down like a bullock from a butcher's hook.

V. Ezra Pound's 65th Birthday
                         October 30, 1950

You call St. Elizabeth's bughouse, hellhole, but you
must be happy enough. A room of your own where
you can type at any hour, there is time for chess,
you play tennis. Fifteen at a time, reserving their hour,
visitors are a constant, streaming over to you, a lotus
on the lawn while you feed squirrels. Raggle-taggle,
the young who call themselves poets do not know
titles of your poems. You mesmerize them anyway
with syllables rapid as Fred Astaire tap dancing along
the canals of Venice. Center stage you never tire
of quoting *In a Station of the Metro.* Richard Burton,
you roar, *The apparition of these faces in the crowd; /
Petals on a wet, black bough.* Don't describe yourself
as broken by prison, clutching at support to stay
despair. I don't want to hear about *magic moments*
you create: filling a glass of water to form a prism so
sunlight will give life color, separate blue and yellow;
a mother wasp artfully building her nest; white-breasted
birds perched on wire that are half-notes on a music staff.

VI. Ezra Pound's 66th birthday
                                        October 30, 1951

Your green land erasing my waste land, how can you
Make it new at St. Elizabeth's? Ezra, on one television,
buttons are gone; an aide turns volume up, then down
by sticking a table knife in a metal slot. Enough. I write
to celebrate, give a gift of your words written while
in your cage outside Pisa: *What thou lovest well remains,
the rest is dross.* On my last visit, we were able to talk
before our hour was over. Twenty minutes to sort years,
flashing like minnows in a school, as we walked back to
your room. Always mixing metaphors, nothing was new
between us, we still had the same feel for text, narrative,
connection of everything with everything else: paint
blooming on the dining room ceiling dropped to petal
the floor like white lilacs after a storm, pasting grass
with confetti; touching a branch heavy with rain was
private, a shower. Almost as if there was blood between
us, our tongues loose as old sinews, I quit bitching about
that morning's traffic, you about cold eggs, late mail.

VII. Ezra Pound's 67th birthday
                                        October 30, 1952

What good does it do for me to visit you, to speak
of your Bollingen Prize in 1949, Frost, MacLeish,
our efforts to free you from typing behind barbed
wire. If I thought I'd get the upper hand, I'd quote,
Old men ought to be explorers from East Coker,
but you would counter my onslaught, say it takes
patience to sort out a snarl. I can just hear you
leading me through the stages. 1.) Loosen all jams
and open a hole through the mass at the point where
the longest string leaves the jumble. 2.) Wind
the tip out right through the center like a stocking
is rolled and keep the snag open, loose at all times.
3.) Don't pull at the end. 4.) Rather, permit a knot
to unfold itself like the pattern of the world that
may not be finished, that must stay open to untangle.

VIII. Ezra Pound's 68th birthday
                    October 30, 1953

1908, you landed in London with your velvet jacket,
beard flaming, a jungle bird too gorgeous to be caged.
Your mission: change the course of English poetry.
With a generosity rarer than love, you collected money,
paid rent, got reviews, publishers for Joyce, Lawrence,
Frost, Hemingway. You gave Hilda Doolittle her name,
H.D. Even then, you were firing off instructions to
the world, though the world paid no attention just like
your friends who found you the same faithful fascist,
charming, unbearable, warmhearted, foulmouthed
bigot, you are today. We labeled you *Saul, Macbeth;*
you sought out power beyond what was possible, spoke
when you should have been silent. Ezra, why can't I
persuade you to repent for all those who came to ovens
in numbers you could not imagine? Do I need to remind
you of 1944, *The Walls Do Not Fall,* H. D.'s words
for you, for your spirit: *yet the frame held: / we passed
the flame: we wonder / what saved us? what for?*

IX. Ezra Pound's 69th birthday
                    October 30, 1954

Year has mounted year. Nine in St. Elizabeth's.
Surely, Ezra, before you turn seventy, there is
some statement you could now allow me to give
the court? Why not say you were misled, unnerved?
Case No. 58102, the record, you know, will be
held up to generations. There's no need to remind
me that you have held my leather-covered notebook,
have read *Inventions of the March Hare.* I began
those poems just after I turned twenty-one, but
I was old enough to know not to expose fault lines,
publish that interview with Booker T. Washington,
the poem about Bolo. Before I sold my collection
to John Quinn, I razored out every page I wanted
destroyed and gave them to you. I had enough sense
to make amends for reading *Gerontion* in 1943
at a poetry recital. No way for me to deny I knew

of gas chambers, knowing vague is a more dangerous
path for poetry than the arid, I inserted *awareness /
Of things ill done* into *Little Gidding.* Compromise is
not a word you admit into vocabulary, only an ideal
of art, as artist you are *monstres sacres.* Ezra, we have
not been granted moral carte blanche. Sounds of words
can never be more than what they are, than who we are.

X. Ezra Pound's 70th Birthday
                        October 30, 1955

A bookmark for your new decade, I enclose the first
line from the first poem in my first book: *Let us go
then, you and I.* Together, we could sit in afternoon
sun; I'd offer dreams of white birches, wheat bread, pink
dogwood in a bowl to counter sleep that frightens you,
too much a rehearsal for death. There's no need for me
to tell you that the end will be a balm the drowning
receive as they surrender. You would mock me, knowing
that in preparation, I *shall wear white flannel trousers
and walk upon the beach.* I can't masquerade in front
of you. Between us, only the heart can prove orient.

After the First Snow, the Poet Visits Manhattan

Wait for the moon to sculpt the fire hydrant into a statue
of frost. Everyone will be marooned; everything will appear

to have the same weight when covered. It's the regularity,
the sameness, the smoothness that does it. Any solid color

will do: black wool coating a man by Federal Hall, white
steam embracing another on Broadway near Chambers.

Gloved hands mask his face. Snow makes visible shapes
you wouldn't ordinarily see. What could be a car is parked

in front of Trinity Church near Wall Street, but it might
be a tank with gun turrets removed, or an elephant kneeling

for a master to mount. Rags of smoke will steam subway
steps. Inhale, then open your mouth to catch snowflakes. If

you pass trees, they will bow; bent in prayer, shrubs will be
shrouded pilgrims. There is nothing to do. Learn to be wind

as snow swirls. Drifts will rise like bridesmaids, with grace
in measured steps two by two up the aisle. Molded as if by

water sanding *azur* sea glass, curves will have all edges worn
off. Nothing will be hard like throaty Russian consonants.

You might show off more French and spout the color *noir*
to recall the pavement. A virtuoso, you could pontificate

about modern art, compare the radiance of light, its harmony
to Robert Ryman's show at MOMA. Pulled from his hands

by the moon, big white canvas was cold, insistent, bleached
of stained life. Covered with paint or snow, sidewalks have

no muck, stench, gut of dog, or crevice for dropping of horse
to rot where goldenrod seeds might wedge. Flakes of snow

are milkweed parachutes with nowhere to root. Powdered
over, the skin of the earth is made up, with pores filled in

like Garbo's face, forever smiling, forever mysterious. You
will never question it, but may need to find words that will

penetrate such perfection. Whether the cold silence of snow
is crisp or light as shredded sponge, your soles must press

down to leave an imprint. Leaving no scent for a trail, you
may walk for days in the middle of streets emptied even

of shadows, only surrounded by snow that holds the seen and
the unseen. Take away color and there is only beauty, shapes

that might be tin cans, the *Post* tied in bales, a dog, garbage
bags or a woman in a red plaid coat curled as if asleep.

How the Poet Adjusts
the Size of Grief: 6x9, 8x12

It's better to try to get control of it.
— Ted Hughes

Margins: a top, a bottom, a left, a right. Beginning:
February, 1956, walking across South London. Fetters Lane,
a bite on your cheek for a kiss, reciprocity of pain, pleasure,
October, 1962: an ending. Ted, was it the twenty-seventh,
your wife Sylvia's thirtieth birthday? Pigeoning into turns
and twists of Devon, your house, surely you knew Sylvia

would not waltz to answer the door. Put red next to green,
Christmas vibrates; no way to attic memory. Collecting
belongings, you might have carried a wooden apple bushel,
already a part of the way you walked, bent over from lifting
Victorias, Pig's Noses, Bramleys. Boxes had splinters you
pulled from fingers pressed to steeple *Spring prayers still*

solid, and save bruised windfall to cider mill for bees to hive
Sylvia's poems. Maybe apple crates were basic to character
of your home, shared like habits, gestures. Painted turquoise,
and red for contrast, you would've coated sides in linseed oil
showing off grain, slowing decay. Towering over the elm
writing table you built, boxes could not be stacked like

bodies spooning night or halves of a clam enclosing a third:
Frieda. Did you repeat Sylvia's line, *Love set you going like
a fat gold watch,* to Nicholas when the midwife slapped him
alive on January 17, 1962. Not a year old, Sylvia carried him
to a Chapham Junction flat. Without you, the family of three
rolled on crackers, eating in bed to stay warm in a cold that

strong armed London. Sylvia's sinuses coagulated, opened
from ammonia on floors, vapor steamed from her nostrils as
she swung a mop in the kitchen at 3 a.m. Always rushing. no
stillness, Sylvia prayed for a mother's helper to outlast needs
of children: *One cry, and I stumble from bed, cow-heavy and floral.*
February 11, 1963: the end. Married four months after your

first meeting in February, dead four months after you left
with Assia Wevill. Symmetry for Sylvia, in language, life:
wet towels stuffed in gaps of doors were margins to contain
smell, the gas, *This dark ceiling without a star.* No words were
tattooed with a needle tipped with blood or ink from her
black Schaeffer pen. Not a drop for Nicholas, Frieda or you.

No time for a life mask, Sylvia's face plastered, straws to
tunnel breath. No paramedic to rip what had already set.
Ready for anything but two glasses of milk she put out, you
must have listened for children thumping like a dog's tail,
something. Did you avoid eyes of tenants, degrees the oven
knob recorded? A quilter squaring off, stitching borders

to turn chaos of scraps into order, did you save broad white
eyelet yoke from Sylvia's blouse, paisley from her skirt, silk
scarf she folded to band brown hair? Cutting out black, gray
like poems in *Ariel,* you kept reds, yellow, green as if you
could paste color on Sylvia's cheeks, cedar her life. Packing
what was now yours, the *mantelpiece mermaid of terracotta*

in lambswool, *coppery fondue pan* in boxes marked *Plath,*
you stacked her poems, journals into other boxes you labeled
Empty. Bedtime stories to cover the children, you edited
your version of Sylvia for Nick: *You are the one / Solid the spaces
lean on, envious. / You are the baby in the barn.* Your hand
gave Frieda daffodils you said you gathered with her mother,

saved her lines: *Your clear eye is the one absolutely beautiful thing.
I want to fill it with color and ducks, / The zoo of the new.*
Their mother, an orchard you fenced, Nicholas and Frieda
picked only your memory of her, read your *Birthday Letters*
to understand why neither smell of their heads, or their hands
on their mother's breast could hold off that night for long.

The Poet Defaces
Sylvia Plath's Gravestone in
Heptonstall, West Yorkshire

To attack it and attack it
— Ted Hughes

A chisel, a hammer, I have come prepared this time.
No need to use a rock, the heel of a boot to hack away
at the *H*. Careful, systematic, Ted, this first letter will be

for poems you cut from *Ariel,* as if a wife's anger,
a wife's damnation could be edited in the heart.
Tackling the *U* for passages in her journals you inked

before publication, I picture you as typesetter removing
leading that holds words apart to set your own text.
No white space for cushion, Sylvia's letters swarmed,

a blackberry *bush of berries so ripe it is a bush of flies.*
I'll get my shoulder into the *G* for the final volume
in her journal you destroyed. An amateur historian

of sorts, deleting one side of the war, you erased
last words like chalk on blackboard, threw away pages
as if deadheading geranium in the wallow of August.

This second *H* is for another journal you say was lost.
Carving blemish from appleskin, gristle digested
by memory, you left Sylvia's *Morning Song* to thicken

like sweet custard for Nicholas and Frieda: *All night
your moth-breath / Flickers among the flat pink roses.*
Working up a sweat, I'm really getting into this *E*

for *Double Exposure,* the novel you mislaid. No fiction,
but your memory, changeable as light, to record Devon,
you were a photographer choosing angle, what to cut

from the frame, say, Assia Wevill's hand on your arm.
Razoring portions of a tape, you could have been one
of the cameraman on Ed Sullivan's show splicing film

to televise Elvis from the waist up. Heir to Sylvia's
poems, you boxed them as HUGHES. The time has come
to let PLATH stand alone. It's just the S I have left to do.

A Poem for David Wevill
by the Poet

No wedding veil but negligee, your wife, Assia, a woman
who invited trespass, surely you realized she had been
married twice before you met on the voyage to Burma.
Was it perfume penetrating as cattails do in weeds near
a spillway or chipped crimson nails that snagged you?
1962, houseguests of Ted Hughes and Sylvia Plath. Devon

afternoons were spent sucking on wine, playing Sing, Say
or Pay. Words somersaulted: moon, a melon wedge; apples,
waterfalls; clouds, a guillotine. Two husbands and two
wives with old quarrels creased as linen. If Sylvia's big,
dark hunky boy, now a man, was twenty minutes late
from a walk, she threw Waterford, their cast iron skillet,

whatever. Ted Hughes was like a first time traveler
in Oklahoma who turns south from Wichita, Kansas,
thinking he can avoid the Great Plains that are flat
as a double edged razor. No matter how far he could
look, his landscape was plotted out, would not be
different, wouldn't get better. Then, Assia. Mongolian

black hair curtaining her neck, wobble of candlelight,
darkness was right for her, a predator with vision
of a screech owl. Their bodies scored at night. David,
suspicion crowded your heart, you turned sullen, plain
in speech. A friend since the fifties when you had met
in Philip Hobsbaum's workshop, perhaps Ted did mean

to stay in his kitchen, unpack sardine tins from two sacks
he dropped on linoleum, but he went off with your wife,
his keys, his wallet. Assia the cape, Hughes the matador,
were you dragged into the bull-ring, pricked into rage?
Wind in argument with water, oceanic fights with Ted,
were inevitable as tide. When Sylvia left Devon, took both

children to London, pillowed her head in a gas oven
after only four months of living alone, neighbors must
have had ordinary curiosity, the village kind over cock
fight bets. To avoid prurient interest in your mismanaged
lives, did you look back, crook your arm into a poem
you might have shared with Sylvia and Ted on a night

they visited "The Group"? *Birth of a Shark* lessoned you
in survival: *He learned this, when they came for him; /
The young shark found his shadow again. / He learned
his place among the weed.* Without you layered as primer
between canvas and paint, Assia couldn't stop rot. Five
years of living with Ted, threads holding fabric of her life

dissolved. An aging actress with smeared lipstick, mascara,
Assia was Sylvia's second act but had a supporting cast.
As oven gas jetted, Assia elbowed the two year old neck
of Shura, the daughter she had with Hughes, a child, David,
you never had. You awoke long before the newspaper
hit the door and brought you into another day: Hughes

in the center of the page, arm lifted as if he were holding
up the tail of a bull. Sylvia was canonized. Your Assia,
her daughter, Shura, not even a footnote. No sheetrocker,
no insulation from feeling, from loss, you gave up your job
as copywriter, London for Spain, stuffing your life into
trunks, trying to empty your heart of what it could not hold.

And Still,
a Bird Is in the Poet

Picasso's fifty-foot high, sixty-two ton gift to Chicago
staring straight at me, I pick the low concrete steps
where Joseph Brodsky sat with Stephen Spender

in the Richard J. Daley Civic Center. Mouths eager,
but no works of art, not made out of Corten to keep
rust from eating them, they would have ignored the night

rain, gotten up and circled Picasso's cables and plates.
First, a horse's head floating out of ribs, its mane
draping to Cleopatra's hair. Next, a woman's profile

that must have reminded Stephen of his wife, Natasha,
who surely was modeled after a bust of Nefertiti.
Rounding the sculpture, its wings lifted them to Daedalus

and Icarus in flight. Was Joseph Brodsky pulled back
to St. Petersburg, the bombs and the sirens, by steel
spreading into the coif of a nun fleeing as his mother did

entering the crypts of the Cathedral of Smolny convent?
Unlike them, I don't move. I'm afraid to interrupt
two boys riding dirt bikes onto Picasso's curved base,

three who bank skateboards to get height for a moment
away from what waits for them on earth. In the center
of the plaza, a fountain has sprays of water that form

a tunnel young girls gauntlet to see who can become
the wettest. It is not water I would mind; for September,
the day is warm. I don't want silk clinging to my thighs

or stomach like their skirts do. With eyes of a hawk,
I hover as the boys do wheelies to lure the five girls
who watch them. Understanding gravity, how it directs

my breasts, I know I can't invent a jump that will not
swing me back to pavement. Filled with a need I cannot
name, I repeat: Joseph Brodsky and Stephen Spender.

The two could not know on that night they shared
in Chicago they would die within six months of each
other. One death was not like the other. New York City.

January 28, 1996. Joseph Brodsky's heart stopped.
He was fifty-five. This number and his death bring
perspective, give this day to me. No longer caring

about underarms that sag, that can't be resurrected,
I take off my shoes, my socks and wade right into
the fountain, my hunger, a song my body cannot sing.

IV

THE POET AS WATER GIRL
FOR SEAMUS HEANEY

Parsley can team up with water and salt
to orchestrate other flavors. Deft at being balmy,
with an exuberance that makes overuse impossible,
parsley is often taken for granted. Imperceptible,
but adding nuance like bubbles in San Pellegrino,
parsley refreshes throats, especially those parched

by reading poetry. With its hint of camphor, citrus
and grass, its subtle peppery bite, parsley cuts fat,
lends a youthful kick, even to potatoes boiled
in Ireland. Able to play the smallest supporting role,
flat leaf parsley can be blunt enough to define a dish,
perhaps tabbouleh. Given top billing, sautéed alone

or with garlic to make the condiment persillade,
it captivates an audience. Often parsley is the secret
ingredient when simmered with onion. Add lemon
and orange zest, gremolata is created, unnoticed,
but essential for ossu bucco. In such sauces, parsley
may seem like just a chorus member or a poet's fan.

In fact, parsley's presence changes everything.

Can the Poet Live
by Bread Alone?

I get it all from earth my daily bread
— Tony Harrison

Imagine, me in England. The White Crusty,
the Cut and the Uncut. The Small Tin,
the Large Tin, the Bloomer. A cottage loaf,

round, white and bouncy like feather pillows,
down filled mattresses, and if the topknot
is missing, I'll be teething a farmer's loaf

dusted with flour. If I finger square corners,
four by eight inches, brown, light, smooth,
not grainy, I will know for sure it's hovis.

Ciabatta, and brioche found their way across
the English Channel. So can I. For a change
of pace, picture me in India. Let's say Bombay

in case *Poets and Writers* wants a caption.
I will stuff chapati, phulka so hot it burns
my tongue, then add to that tandoori nan

and the even sweeter Frontier version,
peshawari nan, into my mouth all at once.
Overloaded? Not until I eat the reshmi roti,

the shirmal, the paratha will I have the need
to confess, and compensate for my sins
of overindulgence. Simplify. Me in Karachi,

Pakistan. With no man servant, backdropped
by dawn, I stand and wait in line all by myself
for a loaf outside Monastery of the Angel's

stone wall. Baked by the nuns to honor God,
the bread is rationed as if there were a war.
No bulk buying even for a poet. Stuffed

with money, my pockets will empty for
bites of crust. A hatch opens. My head must
be bowed, my eyes averted while I file

past, right hand extended just as if I were
a sinner sticking out her tongue like a tray
for communion's grace. A wooden board

slides out with my allotted bread, white,
soft, light like the wings of an angel surely
will be, floating me to what heaven can be had.

WHAT THE POET LEARNS
EATING AN ARTICHOKE

Precisely what draws me to foods, to words
that must be cracked, pried open, puzzled apart?
The artichoke, for example, offers no tropical ease,
doesn't fulfill dreams of extending my hand
from a hammock to pluck mangos just to nibble
or lick, ignoring the juice on my chin, and flesh
clinging to hairy seeds. It must be the ratio of effort
to reward that lures me. To spend so much time
peeling off so many leaves for a piece of pale
green mush is an indulgence like writing poems
that generate wastebaskets of paper for a few words.

Artichokes don't give themselves away to greed
or incompetence. They have to be approached slowly;
their quality of refusal must be listed to be understood:
complicated treasure-box; haughty, elegant courtesans;
or rare peacocks whose feathers are not easily glimpsed.

Other foods such as oysters, crabs, pomegranates
and coconuts require a strategy. Few, however, lend
themselves to out and out revenge. Forced to house
and feed Germans in World War II, the French steamed
only enough artichokes for the troops in order to leave
the Nazis utterly at a loss. With no hosts to imitate,
the soldiers choked, chewed through every bristle, leaf
and thorn. Granted, it was a small act by a powerless
people, but satisfying as legumes can be, sprouting
to a pea that bruises, a bean that climbs to a castle.

Even fewer vegetables lend themselves to psychological
analysis, but I can tell a lot about a man by the way
he eats his artichoke, with leaves strewn about or stacked
in neat piles. Banished from the garden, cast out into

a forbidding world, I can locate delicacies in the most
unlikely places: juice of a prickly pear; truffles under
oaks, or meat of black walnuts, hard to crack, with husks
that stain white gloves. It's an artichoke, nonetheless,
that inspires me to write poems that explore poignancy,
woman's fall from Eden. Occasional but exquisite,
a taste of pure pleasure is compensation, but even dipped
in butter laced with lemon garlic or drizzled in olive oil,
what an effort it is to strip incisor widths of flesh from
the tips of leaves just to make it all the way to the heart.

The Poet Contemplates
the Stinking Rose

I must admit it's the oxymoron of garlic's folk name
in ancient Rome that woos me, not the history.

Rubbed on bodies by legionnaires to ward off colds,
native to the Caucasus, worshipped by Egyptians,

bulbous cloves were shields for the evil eye, thwarted
devourers of blood— vampire, bacteria or mosquito.

In 1652, Nicholas Culpeper recorded garlic healing
bites of mad dogs, ridding children of worms, curing

the plagues, earaches and abscesses. What a choice:
halitosis or teeth marks on my neck. I suppose it

depends on the situation. When Satan stepped out
of the Garden of Eden after the fall of man, garlic

sprang up from the spot where he planted his left foot
and onion from under his right foot. Surely, Satan

did not worry about his breath and would have been
a match for Dracula any day. Garlic's raw sting

sweetens with heat and might have cleansed acid
of the apple on Adam's tongue or could it have been

the aphrodisiac quickening his thighs? Hard to figure
out as original sin, truth does not always announce

itself, can be waiting like garlic in ditches or trenches
by the side of the road. Questions about good and evil

are as difficult to answer as it is to remove parchment
that separates knife from clove. Why garlic can even

surprise a poet who's used to lifting the veil, laying bare
the inside; Percy Shelley wrote from Italy to a friend,

*What do you think? Young women of rank eat—you will
never guess what—garlick!* Shelley did know that sucked

dry of juice, of flavor, of emotion, poems are like prunes,
predictable. With garlic you never know—too little water

when it's growing can invite disaster, too much rain when
the garlic is mature will ruin the crop. If a farmer has

a poet's soul, she stays on an existential edge, will bend
into a hairpin to straighten untidy piles of garlic, because

like muddled lines, stems labeled *scapes* get tangled.
Fleeting as inspiration can be, garlic lasts six months,

will dry out to papery dust, its inside becomes hollow
or even moldy. Thinking of doing a first draft while

planting garlic, I stick cloves in a furrow, don't worry
if they are sitting straight—they will right themselves,

posture perfect. Soft-neck Asian, Turban Chengdu,
California Early, or Russian Red, all I know for sure

is that since I've upped my garlic intake, I haven't been
pestered by vampires—or for that matter, anyone else.

An Ode on a Beet
by the Poet

All ye need to know
— John Keats

I boil raw beets for the pleasure
of it, the old way of it, the work of it,
curly green leaves whistling
to bloody veins. Sunflowers race
for sky, and untrellised, peas languish,
but beets survive shade of cucumber
planted too closely. Into yoga, beets

don't fight for space, or compete
with zucchini. Beet nubs heave,
grow, big or tiny, fissure at the neck.
Large beets peel naturally, small beets
are reluctant, not ripe. Greens steamed,
nubs boiled, cold garnet liquid saved
for dye, wanting this world to be
enough, I leave a taste of dirt, of earth.

It's Blue Sailors
for the Poet

No sense in fishing to throw back fish. Eat
what you catch, my mother insists. Crumble
left over cornbread, roll the oval of sun that
rainbows the dock. Flat eye, unblinking
silver bullet, can't penetrate her heart. Clublike,
the sunny's head is shaped like Indian flint
her father plowed from Kentucky fields. Gills

open and shut, like our love, a trap that can draw
blood. Needing praise, understanding, I transform
battered fried fish into crinolines resting on stays,
explain eating a life I have pulled out of water
is not like tomato, cucumber salad from my garden.
Too late, I realize I've opened another door.
Plant only what I can eat, not borders of green

feathers, cosmos pink and purple, useless just
like the blue of delphinium. Lilacs growing
wild by the shed were good enough to fold into
her grandmother's hands when she was laid out
in the front parlor, chunks of ice in zinc tubs
to keep the body fresh. Not quite eight years old,
my mother took her turn sitting to keep cats

away from her grandmother who didn't thrash
about, gave as little trouble as she could, dying late
on Saturday so she could be buried on Sunday.
Referee for our fights, my father reminds me what
with her own mother working so hard, no indoor
plumbing and all, my mother never had much
petting. Her father sold her goose, Clover,

to neighbors and their son laughed about fat
smoking up the house, breasts he ate Christmas Day.
No time left from work, the Depression, she
ate lard sandwiches in school, wore feed sack

underwear held up by elastic from an inner tube
that couldn't hold another patch. It's too late
for her to write a poem that serves no purpose;

wind off Long Island Sound snakes her shirt
only while she stands drying her hair. Wanting
to show my mother how I love her by recalling
life on the farm, I describe the moon, rising rib
by rib, ploughing a golden furrow into the cove
at Morgan Point. My mother allows as how
she wanted to loop around in circles like a bee,

but was weighted down by feathers of chickens
she pulled apart four days out of seven. What was
I thinking when I took her with me to Shop Rite
to buy endive? Seeing the price, my mother asks
if I'm the Queen of Sheba. Waving the dictionary
like a semaphore, she points out endive, young
leaves of chicory coloring our marsh. I give up,

let my mother pot chicory stems in the cellar.
Teaching me to roast then grind roots to stretch
coffee, my mother's proud of pinching pennies
I won't stoop to pick up, brags how chicory got
her through the morning if egg money ran out.
I question her about being young, being in love.
More chicory. Called Blue Sailors, the flower

sprang up by rocks where a maiden died
waiting for her love to return from the Pacific.
No transplanting, chicory made up its own mind
like my father. His eyes, wild as the weed, brave
blue, were always hungry for her cooking. Letting
her know he was coming from the barn to wash up
for supper, my father's whistle ribboned the wind.

EVEN THE POET DESERVES
A BREAK TODAY

You are a small girl sitting by the window waiting for me
to pick you up. It is cold, it is raining, it is dark, I am tired,

but not too tired to dramatize big news about Arch Deluxe:
The discovery of a new dish does more for human happiness

than the discovery of a star. I ignore the only other quote I
can remember from *The Physiology of Taste* by Brillat-

Savarin: *The cries of the new born babe beg for his wet
nurse's breasts.* We drive straight from Kiddie Korral

to McDonald's. You order a Happy Meal; you smile again.
McDonald's heals. A Big Mac never does disappoint you,

is never late. It's not the best, but always the same pleasure
of unfastening a paper collar and watching lettuce burst

the sides. It's fun, messy, it's childlike. When you can eat
a whole Big Mac, you will be grown up and won't have to

get out of our car early in the morning when I drop you off
like a bag of laundry so I can work on poems. Precocious

at two, you recognized the golden arches. To boast I read
to you each night, I quote history from a Happy Meal about

Ray Kroc, how he bought out McDonald brothers. I recite
numbers to establish your math skills: 11,400 McDonald's

in the USA, 7,000 in 89 other countries including Croatia,
63 in China, two each in Bulgaria and Andorra. Multiplying

at that rate, someday you'll be no more than four minutes
from McDonald's. We eat, I trace our summer car trip,

by circling routes by the McDonald's on the place mat. No
country ham, red eye gravy, or beaten biscuits, we won't

know if we're in Kentucky with grandparents, in New Haven
with pizza, fried mozzarella or in Greenwich, Connecticut

where *ragout navarin* and *haricot* just mean burgoo or stew.
Everywhere is the same if we're at McDonald's. You can't

wait to grow up; you'll bring your daughter to meet Ronald
adding another link onto the golden chain of happiness.

WHY THE POET UNWRAPS
THE CELLOPHANE

Self-righteous with stories of the sow that ate her young
in a sty plastered with dung, my father said pigs were smart,
that when she was eating, she knew. I could see they were
vicious right until a sharp blow on the back of the head
with an axe. Their slaughter was never the dull routine
of cattle who died without making sounds. Like blackberry

thorns, hog squeals were hard to pull out, unlike a knife
plunged to jugular at Aunt Hazel's command, *Stick 'im right
in th' goozle'ere.* Sanctimonious is how I'd describe us as
a stake sharpened at both ends was put between tendons
and front feet to hold the carcass. We hoisted the hog full
length into a barrel of boiling water to get bristles out.

The head was twisted off and brains were scooped out to fry
with eggs for breakfast. Finally, there was real satisfaction,
a climax: one cut down the belly spilled the red, shining like
ebony. Warmed by exhaust from a Ford tractor, we would
trade techniques: hogs should be killed late November
on a full moon or just about. While the moon waned, meat

would shrink with too much lard and during a new moon,
there wouldn't be enough grease. A slice in a pan would
puff up, spit in my eye like an adder. Hogs we didn't kill
were taken on Saturday to Elizabethtown, but only when
the moon was growing so meat would hold water and weigh
more. Eating held such significance; a reputation was made

on curing ham. Doc Hall Pyrtle used five pounds of salt
for a two hundred pound hog. My father liked eight pounds
per hundred mixed with black and red pepper and at least
a quart of molasses. Neighbors buried hams in bushels
of corn or hickory ash, but ours were wrapped in layers
of gauze with red stain seeping through like a shroud.
Swinging on hooks, shoulders hung aloft. When peach
trees bloomed, hams were put flat side down on bare

ground. Cured for two years, unveiling was a ritual, until
we reached the hard brown fat that was far too tempting
to use as an altar for kneeling. Forty years later, I read
New Haven, Connecticut on *The Register* each morning

not Howe Valley, Kentucky. Too many relatives have passed
away since I moved up North to marry. I should label myself
Yankee, buy plots in Beaverdale across from my office.
My father's scythes, mauls and buckets are detail for poems;
the tool shed, part plank, log and chinking is a symbol for
dirt farming. I think about our hogs as I wheel narrow aisles

of Ferraro's Grocery eyeing each Christmas ham. Stacked,
pigs ears sealed in plastic bags, ten cents per pound cheaper
if bought in bulk, or feet split down the middle and crossed
like hands of the dead aren't tempting me. Pork tails are too
much of a bargain to pass up. No salted crust, shrink wrap
keeps swarms of flies, mounted like polished emeralds, off

the rind. Connecticut law requires unwrapped meat to hang
behind walls. Doors are pushed open when I ring a buzzer,
then they swing shut. Is the butcher I invent testing a blade?
Cutting is done in a hidden room; I picture walls inflating
to red balloons. Leaning to hear slaughter pen bawling,
laughter filters through. I parrot words about women who

live years without meat. Pulling me off my pedestal, I hear
Aunt Hazel: Buy what oozes under the plastic. There must be
blood pooled somewhere. Looking in corners, on counters
where it might have thickened, I want a shudder that goes all
the way down my neck, but orange prices plaster windows,
block my view, quench a vision of the hog, wild then stilled.

THE POET BAKES THE PERFECT PIE

1.   Get in the mood. Sing all the verses of Don McLean's *American Pie*. If you lack a voice, inspiration, topic, or setting, if like Don McLean, you *Drove your Chevy to the levy but the levy was dry,*

2.   knead out balled anger until it thins into compassion by preparing dough for a pie. Never get mad at dough. Treat it tenderly. Once you understand texture with your hands, the dough will tell you everything you need to know, and like a Ouija board, offer you

3.   nuances. What it takes to achieve a tender crust is the opposite of what it takes to make a flaky one. Crisco is the easiest and most reliable, but experiment. Lard crusts, hot-oil crusts, all butter crusts could be like working a word into a poem you have never been able to use, but one you like—maybe *tintinnabulation.* Mantra it to soothe yourself while you

4.   tighten, while you cut. Like a layering a triolet, it is tricky to create a flaky crust. Combine chunks of very cold fat rapidly with flour because warmth from your hands can melt it too soon. If fat and flour are not flattened, big gobs of melting lard like an obvious rhyme will leave holes. Above all

5.   avoid sentiment. Dip into passion. An initial blast of heat will result in an evenly browned rim. Dusting some graham cracker crumbs on the bottom of the pie plate will keep the crust from getting soggy, but allow it to stay tender like a poem should be,

6.   considering the human condition. Do not forget generosity of spirit, the importance of largess. There is absolutely no point in putting together a pie, or an homage for that matter, if you are going to skimp on the fruit. Be a Betty Crocker, aim for

7.   immortality. When you bake a pie, you pledge allegiance to red, white and blue, gingham aprons, to a straightforward, simpler way of life. Cookbook or *Norton Anthology*, bridge two generations, and you will have been the poet carried from one century to another, tucked right under an arm, all boxed and ready for picnics in Edgewood Park.

AN ITINERARY FOR THE POET

So alone, you write, *Lord. Sometimes, I'm pleased*
this is our only life. It's not as if you need to structure
a sonnet every day but writing *love* would be harder
for you than chiseling a headstone. My solution?
Head for the armpit of Florida; workshop your senses.
At Cape San Blas, a fishhook of sand snagging
the Gulf of Mexico, we'll drive north on Rt. 98, even
though the first ten miles will be empty beach

screened by cabbage palms, pines, edged with water
layered in green, turquoise, slate and brown. Off
the horizon, thin and dark, a line of barrier islands
can become a metaphor for your heart. Keep an eye
out for life, alligators crossing from the right, snakes
or turtles on the left. Smell palm rot, oyster shells,
low tide, shrimp boats. For no good reason you can
think of, fill your mouth with Carrabelle, Sopchoppy,

Panacea, Tallahassee. At Big Bend, mangrove swamps
will pull out beads of our sweat. Air, thickening
to Jell-O, will lure sandflies and us to white sand,
fine as flour, that my father used to barrel, ship up
to Kentucky for square dances in our barn. If you
still feel lonely, create a family by doing a prose poem
using names of hurricanes: Camille, Opal, Kate.
Like distant aunts without uncles, there is more

than one story for each of them, detailed by houses
on one side of the road, foundations on the other,
washing machines in shallow water that keep
company with air-conditioning compressors, patio
furniture, kitchen cabinets. For a change of pace, we
will turn off main roads, float down the Wakulla River
where life is how you want it to be — no surprises.
Water is clear, every rock in the riverbed can be seen.

Steering the boat, you'll feel secure enough to define
fecund for a dictionary: deer, osprey nests overhead,
night herons, anhingas drying wings in cypress trees,
Spanish moss, wood ducks, grebes. Circling home,
take the Oyster Route, but be prepared to give up
control to taste, to touch, to smell. Bolster confidence,
quote Eliot's J. Alfred Prufrock: *And sawdust restaurants*
with oyster shells. Repress*, restless nights in one-night cheap*

hotels. Your first stop is Posey's in St. Mark's: fishermen
in white rubber boots, crackers, five kinds of sauce
for pearly-gray oysters just tonged up with a wooden rake
from the bay. Actually, Posey's has cleaned up its act,
serves smoked mullet on cardboard instead of blue
gas-station towels. Pre-historic looking, the mullet
bends plastic forks. Be a cave man, don't use one.
No need to use your sleeve, wipe your mouth on napkins

kept on every table. Even if you are still afraid of falling,
dance the two step, the reel, jitterbug, twist, or macarena
in the hall overlooking the river, but remember there's no
chain link to keep you from cannon-balling through screens
into the water. After the second dozen oysters, you should
move on to Boss Oyster in Apalachicola. Ignore the roll
of brown towels, suck or lick your fingers in between
each course of steamed blue crabs, heads-on-shrimp,

hand cut onion rings and barbecue out of the pit. Pitcher
after pitcher of beer will have cups of floating ice. Judge
how sber you are by naming shrimp boats: Rosa Marie,
Marla J, Nixie, Bay Wolf. Our poetry workshop will
be over when you can't pronounce *aphrodisiac* for oyster.
The trip will be complete if you see mermaids lounging
by your table on shells piled into mounds the size of a mall,
if you can finally embrace *the mermaids singing, each to each.*

What the Poet Can Preserve

Chopped, a preserved lemon stuffed right up
a duck's cavity will infuse perfume into the flesh.
Too risqué for me. At seventy, I have to draw
the line somewhere. Now, while I'd like to recall
exuberance of my youth—twisting the night away—

my spine, a xylophone, calls for a beat more mellow.
I might write poems about Persian marketplaces
or Jemaa el Fna, a souk in Marrakech, fantasize
about a cobra dancing to the sway of a wooden flute.
By passing water sellers with wooden chests covered

in dangling brass cups, I could say I headed straight
for goat heads, sheep feet and live chickens. Not
into fiction, I'd better settle for saffron, green tea with
mint, olives. Back to reality, if I still crave preserved
lemons, their taste of wisdom mingled with youth, I

might try recipes for spicy pepper harissa sauce, bulgar
and asparagus, fettuccine with roasted garlic. With
a taste of experience, role models for a poet, preserved
lemons are subtle and they are kind unlike fresh
skinned lemons that cause me to wrinkle my forehead

into a frown. Even with vegetables like zucchini
and asparagus, even spaghetti, whole grains of wheat
and rye, preserved lemons do not act out. Like revision,
there is no hurrying a lemon ripening in a liquid that
takes less than ten minutes of preparation, but at least

thirty days to mature. Force emotion onto a page
or a warm pickled flavor into a lemon by cutting
without restraint, and membrane beneath the skin
will rupture. Magic markers in hand, I learned
blue and yellow create green. Like colors, primary

flavors mixed together produce a sensation with no
resemblance to the original. Details for a ghazal
with its element of longing, lemon juice mixed
with salt, bay leaves and cardamom create a taste
that has more power than individual parts. Exerting

strength in subtle, mysterious ways as my couplets
ought to do, forgiving, preserved lemons soften
a dish, even mutton stew. As if meditating, aged
in brine for months, they learn to find inner beauty
the innocent flesh of a lamb does not have. No need

to force tears or be acidic, reconciling disparate flavors
to mitigate richness that can be like too much sentiment
in a poem, preserved lemons linger first on the tongue,
mouth and then like memory of my mother, my father,
those I loved while on this earth, lodge in the heart.

SEEDS NOT THE POET'S
WORDS PLANTED CROPS

I've come back, Uncle, though to a day I didn't
        want to see. I walk all the way around
        your porch, a tunnel like the stands out
on the road where you laid corn in double rows

and piled up the tomatoes I sold for you. I lean
        over and touch your face boxed in ivory
        silk. You never once said *love* or
to come back here so I would see what death

will look like if death will wait this long for me.
        Maybe it's true that the dead
        return in dreams with messages, but
you won't, tougher than the calluses I still can

feel on the palms of your hands. At Grandma
        and Grandpa's golden anniversary,
        we played blind man's bluff. *It*,
I groped for my cousins who had already gone

back into the house. Never once telling, you let
        me search, calling to the dark, until
        I stood crying in the back field.
What can I do to get back at you, to pull the word

from your set lips that I still need to hear. A solar
        eclipse, giving no light, needing none
        I tried to be you. Hearing and seeing
without thinking like or as, you never looked up

or back or even on when you plowed, saying only
        that corn didn't invent itself. Uncle,
        you had no need to label, certain
furrowed ground would shift from brown to green.

UNEARTHING A VERB
FOR THE POET

It's not sting of cilantro or bite of fresh mint but basil
    that makes tomatoes sing. No need for lemon,
    anise, cinnamon, dark opal or purple ruffle to show
your sophistication, plain old sweet basil will do. History

offers you clues why: tenth century Chinese cultivated
    it; Hindu gods Krishna and Vishnu regarded
    basil as sacred and in Greek, *basilikon* meant royal.
Dueling, the emotions of love and hate surrounding

basil since ancient Rome are found in Keats' heroine,
    Isabella, who buried her murdered beloved's head
    in a pot of basil and watered it with her tears.
There are easier ways to grow it. In *To Emilia Viviani*,

the distraught lover received a gift of mignonette and
    sweet basil, *Embleming love and health, which*
    never yet / In the same wreath might be. Would
Shelley have revised this line if Mary had known basil

adds a warm peppery flash to soft macerated berries,
    or that like potatoes, basil is an aphrodisiac? Basil
    is sunny, basil is affable. Tear it by hand. Eat it raw.
Get a little crazy: add garlic, pine nuts, olive oil, Parmesan.

Pound basil in a mortar for your lips that will O, sucking
    linguine dripping with pesto. Not just an echo, more
    than herb, basil is bold. Rows may replace high school
Memorial Day bands. Don't chop, boil, you'll overwhelm

your sauces. Its essential oils in microscopic hair like sacks,
    basil can dissipate like dreams do exposed to heat,
    heavy knives or acidity. Words of warning: memory
can be banked in a safe. When ingested, leaves of basil will

be tumblers clicking open the past. Stunning to senses,
    sweet as honeysuckle or lilac with heart shaped leaves,
    like love, the smell of basil, the taste of it never had
a thing to do with words, can't be extracted like your teeth.

 V

WINDOWS OPEN
FOR THE POET

Painted shut, warped, no money to replace
them, what am I to do but razor panes,
smooth abused edges, and rebuild frames
too rotten to strip and sand. Casements,

layered like a cave with skeletons of mice,
are my childhood diary. No screens, my mother
sealed these windows to shut out night, cicadas
ratcheting, pollen and dust. No poetry in her,

steering me through every page, every adventure
of Nancy Drew, she didn't want me to repeat
her mistakes, tried to keep me away from men
who lived to carry a gun into the field. Moated

in the basement by lathes, drills, my father taught
me how to worry with boards. Stroking wood,
I was freed from heroines, books marked: *Read*.
I liked sanding tables and chairs because it was

a secret like poems that I kept from my mother:
days of hidden labor that no one but my father
and I would ever understand. Change, revelation
comes, not just at crossings. My father and mother

are dead. I am able to pull out each and every
rusted pulley wheel, and the counterweights,
black canvas sacks I watched my uncle stuff
with lead shot, tie off with rope. There is a way

of making this long story end: my windows will
slide up, then slide down at a touch, unzippering
my life. I'll be on the lookout for crape myrtle
to explode, wisteria, even a trumpet vine to invade.

The Poet Courts Electricity

I don't like verbal or visual fireworks. Why do I court
    static, skate feet on shag rugs until fingertips live wire?
    I understand why I rub balloons on my head,
    stick them to the ceiling. I want to be in demand
as a birthday party guest. Sometimes just to fool

myself into thinking I'm trapped like a lizard
    in a jar, I put on a turtleneck. When I'm good
    and ready, I stand before the mirror
    in a dark room and palm my head. If voltage fizzes
up and out of my hair like carbonation in champagne,

I award myself a Girl Scout badge. Socks fresh
    from the dryer don't give me the charge I get
    out of running my fingers along the TV screen
    to shock my brother and his girlfriend. Defusing
them, I come up with a scientific explanation: sketch

polarity and electrons on our blackboard, label static
    electricity an impersonal force of nature I can't control,
    even in a poem, only work with for a time the way
    FDR did two-stepping with Stalin. If I cross
a room, reach to switch off lights, a veil of sparks leaps

out, circling my wrist until my hand is even bluer
    than my lips when I dive into the pond out in back
    by the livestock barn. Grabbing a fistful of mud
    and weeds to anchor me, I stay down as long
as I can. Letting the bottom suck me in until my ears

are a bomb, I toy with exploding, with sleeping forever
    bagged in water. Knowing there is surface, I scissor
    kick, pull with one arm, spearing through the skin
    to air, to light with one hand, the other hanging
onto what blackness can be held from the water's depth.

The Poet in Last Light

Pack up your gear, head for The Quinney Quencher
    if you haven't speared a sturgeon ice fishing
      on Lake Winnebago. Chug the house specialty,
a beer with a minnow in it. Required: a dark shack,

one big hole and the willingness to stare for hours.
    Let go of all the adjectives you've been saving
      to use in poems for *boring*. Describe looking
up your chimney waiting for a duck to fly over or

your father in Joshua Tree living seventeen years
    watching for a nolina in his side yard to
      bloom. Desert people know how to wait
for magic, for a flower that is not minor, that is not

common. Some years, hillsides of nolinas send up
    spikes as big as a leg. When the bud unfolds,
      it's the size of a family Christmas tree like
those discarded evergreens marking roads plowed

by Otter Street Fishing Club into grids crisscrossing
    Lake Winnebago. Twenty inches of frozen
      water and 3779 shanties will give you faith
needed to walk on ice. Sturgeon avoid light; paint

inside walls of your shanty black. No windows, sun
    on the ice outside will give you illumination,
      a yellow-green glow from an opening about
the size of a kitchen table. Waiting, hum the theme

from Beethoven's last piano sonata, the one where
    you imagine him looking through the bright
      entry of the world into the dark. It's illegal
to drop bait for a sturgeon. Sit over the hole, jiggle

decoys and wait for the fish's natural curiosity to
        surface. For lures, you can carve a wooden
        walleye, weight it with lead or your brother's
plastic pipe dripping with mirrors and plastic figures

of Sesame Street's Miss Piggy and Cookie Monster.
        Willing to experiment? Dangle an agitator
        out of a Maytag washing machine, Styrofoam
coffee cup or even a bowling ball painted green with

pink spots like Brett Olson who has speared fifteen
        sturgeon, his quota of one a year, since he
        turned fourteen. Brett swears his catch all
came in so fast, they headed the bowling ball and

rolled over. If you do sight a sturgeon, drop the spear
        hanging from the ceiling. Like learning to show
        not tell, spear fishing is about trusting your eight
foot twenty pound shaft. Attached to 50 feet of nylon

rope, its tips should hang under the surface, disengage
        so your dinner can't pull away. Don't become
        discouraged. Like the bloom of the nolina,
the sturgeon is worth the wait. Syd Groeschl has tried

for fifty years; Tom Springborn has had no luck for
        nineteen. Both know their trophy must be right there
        beneath them. Hands cramp not from writing but
waiting for five feet and a hundred pounds. Like seeing

your name on a page, it's the chance to prepare one, taste
        smoke from their own wood that keeps them
        crossing Wisconsin ice each winter. That and having
their picture taken weighing in for the cover story

in *USA Today*. Camera shy, for you the appeal is that
        the sturgeon is so old and has been swimming
        through dinosaurs, wilderness, other predators in
silence, tireless as a glacier for 150 to 200 million years.

Resting under your feet, it offers a way to absorb part
     of your past and frees you from having to visit
     mounted skeletons in the Smithsonian. Hooded
in bone, lessons about survival are trapped by coded

cells in this fish that has swallowed flesh of centuries.
     Learning patience by revising poems, and from
     your father who saw a nolina bloom, it's enough
for you, that in the darkness below, your prize is waiting.

No Creel Limit for the Poet

The wind must have forgotten. It's August.
    There's that Long Island chop;
        fish are everywhere. Snappers are

in, roiling scalloped waves as shiners leap
    into silver fireworks, cascading
        onto the shore. I'll whip the boat

to full throttle! No putt, putt or hanging
    over the stern to drift, casting in
        Vermont ponds black with pines.

I want wake, spreading to angel wings.
    There must be sound, splashing,
        slapping, more than a line arcing,

more than the hiss of a swan. I won't relive
    last week with no wind to shunt
        away humidity, dilute mugginess

or ruffle the skin. This spot is guaranteed,
    no need to throw in bait the size
        of quarters in St. Barnabas' collection

plate. Solid as words filling page after page,
    the blues will hook themselves
        and jump right up into my boat

if I don't catch them. I may have been
    searching for answers in poems, for fish
        that were not around, but today

they are on the surface, floating almost into air
    for gulls to snatch without calling,
        without diving, without getting wet.

Ice Fishing in Minnesota
with the Poet

You're in walleye world if, as thoughts about poems
    grow strange, you forget you failed basic math.
    Drive past rows of fish houses on Mille Lacs.
With ice three feet thick, 200 square miles adds up

to 17 billion cubic feet of ice. If one foot weighs
    about 50 pounds, ice totals 850 billion pounds,
    in mammal units, the equivalent of 53 million
mature African bull elephants. Add two feet of snow,

times 200 square miles. Remember moisture varies.
    Hard to say how much that snow weighs.
    You call it a lot. Maybe 348 billion pounds,
or 22 million more elephants stampeding Mille Lacs,

already burdened with 5,000 ice houses with anglers,
    pickups, snowmobiles, generators. Stop!
    Get a grip. Mantra Henry David Thoreau's
Simplify, simplify. Appeal of a fish house is cobbling

found wood, fulfilling rectangular fantasies in plywood,
    chipboard, scrap paneling. You could be right
    back in Harlan County with your uncles, gathering
as if they were holding a construction convention about

outhouses or in a Hooverville from the Great Depression.
    Revise. Cut back! Borrowing an ax and boards
    from an Irish friend's shanty, Thoreau built his home
for $28.12½. The 10 x 15 space was smaller than most

of Minnesota's fish houses. If Walden Pond had not
    been shorn of ice by Hyperborean ice-cutters
    each winter, Thoreau could have towed what
Emerson must have secretly labeled *shack* onto the ice.

Puncturing the skin of Walden Pond to fish for pickerel,
　　Thoreau might never have written about a root cellar,
　　but described his ice hole as a sort of porch at
the entrance of a burrow. Starting to get strange, walleye

again, you can't stop yourself. Calculating Thoreau's
　　weight, you multiply it pressing down on the dark
　　body of Walden. Control gone, you hallucinate:
Thoreau in Mille Lacs, fishing mostly by feel, partly

by sight. Next, it is Thoreau in ice-house hypnosis,
　　with the long distance stare that comes from
　　focusing on what won't focus: the indeterminate
place in a poem where a line trails off into uncharted space.

The Poet Visits
Fair Haven, Connecticut

No longer paved with shells, Pearl Street has oysters piled
      around doors, not crushed to feed the ducks,
      but bleached by one hundred and fifty years

of work in shallows. Built into hills on sides of the Quinnipiac,
      houses front the river, stilled faces lifting lace
      to peer out as they did when Fair Haven led

the world in exporting oysters. Trees hang on the banks, roots
      exposed like the tentacles on squid or the scrub
      pine at the rim of pits left by miners in Harlan County

who were men like my father. Shovel shells, then empty buckets
      and back again was not any different than stripping
      land that surfaced to air not rivergreen water. Fill,

with bits of coal almost blue in the sun, was bulldozed back
      leaving earth not good for anything but holding
      the surface of a family's world together. There is

no smell of sulphur. To detail smell, touch, I wade waist deep
      in the Quinnipiac. It's old hair I smell. No oyster
      crops for light, but darkness, almost a breathing

from remaining beds as if the muck from United Illuminating
      is trying to take over, pooling like shadows
      in the corner of a dirt floor. I come here to hang

over Grand Avenue Bridge so often, my fingers number brown
      chips on the rails; I know which arch the gulls
      prefer. Salt marshes move with the tide, ring

the river's mouth. On sunny days, landfill shines as it washes
        to Long Island Sound, past barges, Lighthouse Point,
        the breakwater. I've given up on sonnets, sestinas but

I still think I can make rocks walk, fall between every third
        ripple, dropping one by one. I never tire of this
        one-sided catch, or spruce pilings with slick creosote

soaked sides, or the air like my mother's arms. At night, I can
        hang my head over the pier and as the moon mirrors up,
        stars are dropped like the sweat on dirt caked faces

of fishermen pushing wheelbarrows overflowing with oysters
        up the Quinnipiac's banks to wives waiting
        in above ground basements to shuck off sharp spines.

As if writing poems, women spent all day forcing briny meat
        to yield, packing oysters in salt which were shipped
        and sold in Chicago, London, New York and Paris.

Pearls they found were strung, twisted twice around their necks.
        Each wore the life her man dug out, beaded in black
        like a miner's lungs or in albino drops of blood.

No Natural Bridge
for the Poet

Four dollars bought a round trip on a sky lift. One half mile,
six hundred feet in altitude didn't sound bad. With my father,
I opted for the ride. Proud to be saving eighty year old pride,
I had not counted on looking down on climbers sweating out
a mile. So there I was, reviewing my fear of height, as cables

lifted us by going right up a cliff. I'd learned to write poems
by looking straight ahead, keeping close to earth. It was easy
to see that I'd have to cover my eyes if I used my ticket back
down. Swaying just enough in our seat, my father recited for
the fiftieth time how his brother fell from a black walnut tree

being cut for cash to keep the farm because he trunk hugged
rather than trusting ropes held to steady him. I didn't want to
hear about formations ribboning Kentucky, but I got geology
lessons anyway on bridge formation. Limestone (CaCO3)
was a sedimentary rock indigenous to Florida and Kentucky.

Embedded with oceanic skeletons and peppered with aquatic
abscesses, it swelled with rain, shrunk with drought to form
sinkholes. Before I closed my eyes for the final hawk-like
ascent, my father pointed out sinkholes by a cave he climbed
in when he was nineteen because the L&N Railroad strung it

with electricity. Sixty years hadn't aged the mountain, just
him. Hostage to the chair's safety bar, I was force-fed native
pride: our bridge was seventy-eight feet long; Gray's Arch
was two feet longer, Whittleton Arch, one hundred feet. I
had come to find the heart I'd gouged right in the middle

of the bridge thirty years ago, just a day after my wedding
in Lexington. Rock was no more lasting than my vows.
The scar my new husband and I carved had worn away. No
way to know what day the last curve disappeared, what boot
ground it out; all I had to touch were three sons born since I

had been there. Turning from the bridge, I could see strength
given to me had been taken from my father, but I would not
get back on that skyway, two dollars per ticket and his pride
be damned! Edging down, we passed pock marked sandstone
I imagined in February covered with icicles, some dripping

over twenty feet. To show off what I'd learned, I recited
lines from *Kubla Khan* by Coleridge: *A sunny pleasure-dome
with caves of ice.* Fat Man's Misery, I told anyone who'd listen,
was what scientists would call a vertical joint fracture with
walls eighty-three feet long and fifty feet high. Looking for

someone in a green park uniform to police one-way traffic,
I worried about getting stuck, swore to diet. With my poet's
lens, Balanced Rock developed from a hunk of sandstone
poised to spring off its narrow stem to a mushroom or an
atomic cloud. Ignoring me, climbers turned around to listen

as my father told how the pedestal rock was called Sphinx
back in 1900 because from the correct angle, it looked like
the one in Egypt. Guidebook in hand, we passed attractions
one by one: niter mine, Devil's Gulch, slowed going down
Needle's Eye Stairway, stopped at Lovers' Leap. Trailing

my father, I forgot the heart I had come to see, the love
I believed would form a natural bridge with a husband born
in South Africa after his parents fled from Nazis in Germany.
Letting my father pretend he was inspecting a piece of pipe,
we paused at a large clearing, a skylight cut by felled trees,

opened by limbs sheared in last winter's ice storm. We
debated: hemlock or pine. Remaining branches were high.
Looking up to needles that were clearly feathering, I knew
how bad his eyes must be. There was a silence I was afraid
to pull like blue yarn sticking out of my sleeve. I could not

resist removing it, and left a dime sized hole in my sweater.
Pushing off a log. I'd already created a symbol out of old trees
making room for new growth; it's nature's way. There would
be no green for my father. No blue spruce, he was shedding
pounds. Surely nothing needed space he was taking on earth.

The only sound between us came from pinecones pulled down by gravity, or gnawed off by squirrels. I looked away from those already melting into the needled floor. I did not pronounce the word *inevitable* only walked ahead of him over the slick parts in case he slipped and started to fall.

THE STEP-FATHER NIGHT
FISHING WITH THE POET'S SON

Linked first by marriage, now by ritual of rod
and hook, weighted by frozen bait, insurance
that my new son and I would never need lures,
Matthew dipped into schools of kellys; to show
him how to secure one still alive by pushing steel
through middle, I describe the blue heron we had
nicknamed *Doctor Doom* for the aim of its bill.

Cradling his hands, I wanted to tell him how I held
him on the ride home a day after he was born, how
his mother and I drank champagne, making love
on Morgan Point the night he was conceived, how
I rushed her to the hospital, how I watched his head
emerge. None of this happened. No odes, no priest
consecrating bread and wine, I couldn't perform
a sacrament transfusing my love into his blood.

I'd have a beer then settle down to wait the arcing
of our lines flung out over the moon. A shining
whipped the night before my son hooked a snapper.
Lashing dark, we kept casting into unfamiliar depths,
until we snagged another then another. If I were
a poet, I might have created a metaphor for my fear
that Matthew would find my ordinary life, my love,
lacked luster in the telling light. Instead, I told him
to gut the fish he catches or it will rot, how to hold
a knife as he cut the fillets for us to grill. Later,
beginning our own tradition, we fed one another
the first bite from the fish we had caught, from
the meal we had created, from the flesh we shared.

THE POET AS EMPTY NESTER

Pulling away to college, his life loaded into a U-Haul,
    no kiss, Matthew's good-bye is physical, playful,
        a punch, a shove into new census box for me to check.
Eighteen years of being his mother, one eye was focused

on the job at hand, the other on this distant day when I
    would be left standing in the driveway with memory
        of what I was losing clinging like lint on my blue top.
Telling myself this end was a kind of peace the dying

know giving up the body, I wave him off as if I were
    swatting dragonflies we chased the summer he turned
        thirteen. Shin deep in a riffle of the Gila River
where tan and yellow cliffs columned like tree trunks,

we grouped with ten other lungers and thrashers armed
    with nets. Spending each night straightening abdomens
        and untangling thorny legs, my son and I labeled
gilded river cruiser, beaverpond baskettail, sandhill bluet,

cardinal meadowhawk. A boy in Japan, not New Mexico,
    Matthew would have tied weights on the ends of silk
        to throw at dragonflies who, with luck, would confuse
the silver for a mosquito, attack, get tangled in thread, be

unharmed. I started a conversation I'd managed to postpone,
    pointing out that two dragonflies joined into a flying
        wheel were mating, a pair of sexual aerobats. The female
deposited eggs in plant tissue while the still-attached male

stood guard, not leaving her as Matthew's father had done
    before he was six months old. Exhaustion staggered
        me. Too tired to catch jokes, always three to four
syllables behind, if I started using words like *responsibility,*

Matthew knew how to distract me. To cut some slack,
    he asked about growing up in Kentucky. I took the bait:
    dragonflies were called *snake doctors* reviving rattlers,
copperheads, Lazarus-like, from the dead, or *devil's darning*

needle stitching together lips of bad children as they slept.
    We learned quickly a dragonfly can't be blindsided.
    Best technique was to pancake. Coming right at me like
a baseball pitch, incandescent red eyes glared and taunted,

first a slider, then curve ball and change-up combined. I held
    the sock of the net against the handle to minimize drag.
    The dragonfly kept coming. White netting whistling air,
I was Hemingway facing the dragonfly eyeball to eyeball.

I'd like to say I let my catch go as black patch pupils stared
    at me. Filling a glassine envelope, first the eyes glinted
    with blue then green brilliance, but longing devolved
from primary colors to mist as deep as a fortune-teller's ball.

I could use one now as I watch my son's brake lights go off.
    How will he get on without my advice about attending
    classes, avoiding beer, sorting whites and colors? I could
preserve Matthew in the study mounted with my collection

of Gila River specimens. Acetone holds enameled colors of
    the abdomen and thorax, but not luster. Eyes, gone from
    opalescent pools to flat opaque, color of rust, lecture:
let dragonflies go, live to burnish air with iridescent wings.

Driving with the Poet's Father in Winter Park, Florida

Unexpected, the rain, sand taking on the depth of slate
in this, a state for tourists, or others like you waiting to be
boxed for the trip home to Kentucky. Spiral of palm, no
coyotes to background, quail to startle, just reek of urine

from needles of tamarisk rooting to hold what cannot be
held, the dunes draining like an hourglass. You point out
the tree's small leaves, like blue-green scales on a fish,
cluster of pink flowers in spiky racemes, feathery as ostrich

plumes. I can't resist teasing with *like father, like daughter.*
Here you are using similes just when I had gotten used
to your bragging about never writing a love poem, never
reciting Longfellow on the gym stage. I'd like to think

that a poem is beating in you, the rhythm ventricled
and pumped into arteries by your heart. You still treat
me like a child, your voice kind, your talk simple, like
the day you didn't want me to see the heifer that slipped

through the fence, got hit on the interstate, bloated, four
legs up like a table on its top. I keep trying to turn talk
to death, afterlife, angels with stiffened wings starched
like the doll your mother crocheted to cover extra rolls

of toilet paper. You remember how we hung on diamond
chain links at the Bluegrass Airport on the weekends,
watching the planes land for something to do at night.
Mother taught me to embroider hankies, but you let me

smoke candy cigarettes while you belted out, *When
the moon hits your eye like a big pizza pie, that's amore.*
Not knowing there was one muse, let alone nine, you
recited order of planets, names of every state flower, bird,

and capital on the road trips I hated. Today, it's as if all
words were stuck back with you in an Appalachian hollow.
Never a one to read books, it's not titles or plots of Twain,
Hemingway or Austen that go, but names for leaves of purple

loosestrife, bull thistle, spotted knapweed. All, invaders
like cancer, crowding out white cells, marrow in your bones.
Their roots, leaves, shoots and seeds run roughshod over
native plants, changing soil, water, landscape, wiping out

microorganisms. Even mammals, warm-blooded like you,
cannot withstand the onslaught. Battling yellow star thistle
and star of mum, both weeds from the Mediterranean
strong enough to kill a horse outright, other farmers outside

Elizabethtown abandoned their land, but not you. There is
always hope, always the statistic. Mats of alligator weed
choking the Everglades have been gnawed into scattered
strands by flea beetles and moths. Who knows what scientists

will find tomorrow? As if the dead have need for clothes,
I pack your suitcase with thermal underwear, a maroon robe
and unfold the wheelchair like Merrywood's daycare
entertainer undoing rice paper wings of origami. I want you

to write a poem for me, to let your heart stay where your body
cannot, but you are down of hawk as I lift you, so light you
will soon soar. I want someone to tell me where you will go.
I want to know that you will not cry out as you sleep.

THE POET'S BOOTS
WERE MADE FOR WALKING

Too young for congregating in the praying corner at church,
you don't want to be stuck in Harlan County forever.
Your husband's done in by the mines, the hoot owl shift.
Black lung got so bad he couldn't do anything but hawk
up gunk. There's got to be another, better town where you

could rake grease back on the griddle. Frying eggs *looking
at you* or *shipwrecked*, you're tired of getting ragged about
the piddling bit of grits you dish up by rolled cigarettes
attached to a lower lip. Puzzling over the license plates
on out of town cars is about as useful as waiting for your

brother to grow a square tomato that'll fit his sandwich.
Any town has this kind of work to offer, coffee to refill.
Take a boat, take a plane. Go to Italy. It's Genoa if streets
go up and down with houses above and below. Get caught
in the rush of wind between them. You are in Turin

if straight streets never end as you look out over railings
of your balcony where a double row of trees fades away
into white skies. In fields of fog, Milan's houses will turn
their backs. It will always be the same room in every town.
Keep your suitcase unlocked, open for the next trip. Stack

your poems in dresser drawers so they are always ready
to be packed again. Dust will smart in your eyes, pocket
stuffed with new last lines, want ads. You will always keep
the look of the first-time traveler until you're seated, back
home, ready for the preacher to shout, *Do I hear an Amen?*

AT MACHU PICCHU WITH THE POET

Pale as a slug, in Peru my face is flushed above a striped
poncho that could have sheltered armies. Black leggings
sprout from folds woven in red, fuchsia, turquoise, hot pink
diamond fringe. Natives know I'm not local, must not

realize I'm a poet because I have to pay to take a picture
of a woman's liver spotted llama. Back-dropped by Andes,
I see why Incas took the mountain route to Machu Picchu
rather than winding the Urubamba Valley. On the Inca Trail,

when I arrive, before I descend, I'll look down on terraces,
pitched-roof houses, stone walls outlining Machu Picchu.
Few places on earth could be worth sleeping on the ground.
To view the sacred city from Intipunku, Gate of the Sun,

where Incas stood to control access to center of the world,
would be. I thought I knew mountains, grew up near
Cumberland Gap that funneled pioneers westward, thrust
some peaks as high as 6,000 feet, but they hadn't prepared

me for the climb. I'd trained for descent by planting corn
in ground that did not yield to half-hearted hoeing. Crops
coaxed from slopes taught me value of what was hard
to come by. A potato was seasoned by fear of rolling

to a ridge's bottom, a broken neck. Going down, from
the trail's highest point at 13,780 feet, I move in a waddle
from left foot to right. I advance, don't stop with both feet
on stair treads like Norma Desmond making her entrance

in *Sunset Boulevard*. Meeting sheer rock, Incas chipped
a split into fifty feet of tunnel I squeeze through like I did
at Fat Man's Misery at Natural Bridge. No one has strip
mined coal, or used these peaks as symbols for anything

but mountains. Looking down on Machu Picchu, I see
what Pablo Neruda didn't climb high enough to see, could
only imagine: *the tallest crucible that ever held our silence.* Raw
like my grandfather's hands, Inca knuckles must have been

badged with scabs from puzzling and chinking boulders
to terrace this amphitheater. Clouds slice power lines. I tip
my porter a day's wage; he wings staircases, my duffel bag
flapping, but I'm in no hurry to stumble down to my hotel

with muscle that has survived. Seeing the road worn flat
as a scar, I pity tourists who are being hauled like steamer
trunks from the railroad station. No five day hike, they have
spent four hours coming from Cuzco, fifty miles southeast.

I also give thumbs down to each helicopter announcing new
arrivals every twenty-five minutes, lifting the faint hearted
who might as well already be in body bags. Standing still
as a blue heron, I forget how I counted each step, each breath

taken on the Inca Trail and hold onto only the entire trek.
In my first schoolhouse, one room in Somerset, Kentucky,
I learned what happens this day, this minute won't decide
my fate, my world. Knowing nothing respects boundaries,

I don't want to break the sacred into rooms, foundations
cracking, walls about to split. A tongue licking at what
would soon no longer be there, this joy, this height, I vow
to see my life as a whole, not measure it out in days, or years

broken into entrance, the end. I may snail forward or spiral,
but I have climbed the trail, walked in steps of the Incas.
I can yield to the ambush of years. This moment of arrival is
a departure. I'll never see Machu Picchu from the top again.

Too Late for the Poet
to Cross Country on a Thumb

At seventy, I admit I still hope to sidle into *Surprise!*, but
not quite like the one a mob created by mounding pyres
with Mussolini's military portraits on top after invading
Case del Fascio on the date of my birth: July 26, 1943.

Still buttoned at collar and cuff, I'm no Edward Hopper
painting *Hotel Room*. I would not leave a yellow letter
creased in the woman's hand, but unfold it for a voyeur
to reveal betrayal, so the words hunching her back are clear.
I will always explain too much, but I am working at being
quiet, trying to witness, not seek the most efficient path
or use *diesel, marco polo* and *arrow* as verbs in my poems.

With wives they love, my sons are not swallows who will
return home. No architect in need of blueprints for a nest,
still, I watch a sparrow fly in and out of a rusted dryer vent
I forgot to seal. Rejecting cellophane larger birds had left
from winter, choosing twigs that are supple, the sparrow
doesn't care if it uses red yarn or finishes last. Steady wings,
patient flight—there's a birthday wish here: *Twig, Twig.*

Would it be foolish to try so late in life for grace of a maple
that releases sail shaped seeds not knowing where they land
or if they grow? Practical for so many years, I'll shuck off
Grandma Todd whose garden was about vegetables to can
and plant a haunt for bees and hover flies of airy clouds of
pink and white thyme. A garden for all seasons, there will be
wooly thyme, mother-of-thyme, and camphor. If I find
a morning when being alive is enough, will it unravel my
heart because I'll be hectored by the thought it might never
come again? I could prepare if only I knew when a day like
a sudden red flame of flower that keeps me from uprooting
vines will come. Only a stupid woman would stand and wait.

An Obituary for the Poet

One I'm writing for myself will not read like my mother's
grocery list. Stacked, cans of prune juice, red kidney beans,
and hominy should form her gravestone with bars of Ivory

soap and Brillo scouring pads for a base. No Kentucky
limestone will do for my mother. Black veined marble will
be chiseled in days she spent numbered by sink, refrigerator

and stove. To flesh out the final memory of myself I plan
to leave for my three sons, to show what a rebel I could
have been, I'll mention the Dixwell Stop and Shop where

I donned a beret, scissored labels, leaving cans looking like
silvered bullets or stove pipes. My mother stood near a shelf
fingering soups, as if the choice of mushroom, chicken rice

or tomato mattered to my father. In the summary of my life,
rather than poems I've written, I'll list melons I've known:
Casaba, creamy white and sweet; a Persian, pink-orange and

spicy; Crenshaw, cross between the two; and as grand finale,
orange fleshed Honeydew. No Jacque Pepin or Gael Greene,
I'll ask *The New Haven Register* to include my grandma's recipe

for jam cake with raisins, black walnuts, coconut, nutmeg,
blackberry preserves, crushed pineapple and her top secret
ingredient of three teaspoons of cocoa. At last, I will dare

to reveal in print the joy I took from each tip of very young
asparagus, teething, then mouthing the stalk whole, and I
had, upon more than one occasion, tongued an avocado, first

yellow then green. Topping my column will be a picture
marked *Early Photo*. On the open deck, I will be on the edge
of a hot tub, buck naked, sucking hairs of a mango seed dry.

EATING CAKE IN THE FRICK
WITH REMBRANDT AND THE POET

It's my birthday and I'm stuck. Wings beating black,
in spite of its insatiable appetite for bluefish, a cormorant
is shocked into Connecticut sky by a private jet roaring
over Morgan Point out of Tweed-New Haven. No one
is coming to fly me in, fly me out. Who cares if I recycle?

Summer's slouching to an end; I should do just one thing
right here, right now but I would rather grind memories.
Why can't I be Rembrandt painting his 1658 *Self Portrait?*
Last spring in the Oval Room, if Frick's guard had turned
his head, I could've caressed rugged brush strokes probing

Rembrandt's aging flesh. His knees almost missing, I might
have ended up on his lap. Mercedes-Benz habits, bankrupt
at 52, his art hawked, his home lost, his cane is still silver
tipped, he is draped in fur. Floppy black velvet hat as crown,
painter's stick as scepter, he is the potentate of his studio.

Probably because like me he is overweight, a wine red sash
is belted high on a golden-yellow jerkin making him look
busty, maternal. Unlike poets, Dutch painters did not use
self-portraiture for personal probing—but was Rembrandt
wondering what his talent was worth? *Self Portrait* could

be a tag sale with splashy, chunky surfaces labeled: outsider,
visionary who is shunned, painting only for himself. Pink
chafe mark on his chin, Rembrandt shadowed his eyes,
spot of white on one ignites drama that smolders within.
I'd have advised him to master ignoring mirrors, move

everything as I did out of the medicine cabinet, strip walls
bare of pictures with glass that dared to reflect a face I did
not recognize, a body I wanted to elongate. Painted with
a splotched hand, ravenous as a cormorant for fame, how
could Rembrandt have doubted his genius? Perfectly lit,

wrinkles in both cheeks have deepened to creases. For me, light's a thief, not a friend. If only I could muster courage, stare in a mirror, maybe I wouldn't see a grey mastodon. No Rembrandt, still I'm in no rush to leave my body, at least not until I blow out candles and lick the last red rose on my cake.

THE PAINTER

for Marcia Ann Harris
June 3, 1939 – March 17, 1989

Parking your wheelchair next to a marble bench in the Met
so I could also sit down, you point out Constable's technique,
his proportion of landscape to seascape and why it was
he began to paint in bigger canvases after marriage. Moving
you on to Gauguin who was on the same floor, a large oil
reminds me of your painting of your father with five friends,

three piggy-backing the other three, with arms doubled around,
fists clutching ties. Black and white unsettled to purple, more
purple darkened to bruise two faces, army green on another.
The six sets of features are starting to tip back, perhaps to keep
insides from spilling. After you couldn't grasp pastel pencils,
you controlled what you could, understanding your MS was

holding your body, a balloon whose string would soon be cut.
Your brother, Ed, stood outside my poetry workshop, crying with
you dead, he was an only child. The cause was starvation you
willed, not MS. Your brother reached for you, straining
his arms to give you legs, fingers strong enough to mix oils,
but his hands passed through air. When your two sons would

not take your ashes to scatter, we stopped cremation. There was
nothing else we could do but bury you back in St. Louis between
your father and your mother. We knew you would be angry
because you couldn't sit out in the car to escape them,
their rising voices. Until he threw the first dirt while I held his
arm, Ed stayed nervous, anxious the mikveh's woman might

interrupt the ritual washing to deny you burial because you
had a green and black spider the size of a half dollar tattooed
above where a left hip bone protruded. Marcia, at your death,
during your life, the spider wove no web, trapped nothing we
could suck juice from to dilute the bitter taste we can't swallow
or spit on the ground. It is floating, floating still in our mouths.